D1611434

Tristram Shandy:
The Games of Pleasure

Tristram Shandy:
THE GAMES
OF PLEASURE
Richard A. Lanham

❧

University of California Press
Berkeley, Los Angeles, London
1973

University of California Press
Berkeley and Los Angeles, California
University of California Press, Ltd.
London, England
Copyright © 1973 by The Regents of the University of California
ISBN: 0–520–02144–4
Library of Congress Catalog Card Number: 70–174461
Designed by Steve Reoutt
Printed in the United States of America

For English 183
UCLA, Winter Term, 1969

Contents

Preface

This essay began life as coda to a much broader survey of Renaissance rhetorical styles *sub specie ludi.* As things that touch Laurence Sterne will do, however, it went on and on. Growing thus into independence, it has in a very real sense left its ancestry behind. I have tried, therefore, in a very brief second chapter to sketch what this tradition was. In ranging beyond accustomed classical and Elizabethan rhetorical preoccupations, I may have overlooked (or unwittingly paraphrased) some pertinent eighteenth-century studies. If so, let me here apologize to the scholars concerned.

The notes reflect my debt to the considerable body of thoughtful Sterne scholarship, a debt no less profound for frequent disagreement. But they do not, perhaps, fully reveal two indebtednesses, one immediate and one longstanding: to the brilliant originality of John Traugott's *Tristram Shandy's World;* and to the inspirational vigor, breadth, and penetration of the writings of Kenneth Burke. Precisely from Burke, indeed, I might take the principal *caveat* such a study as this ought to provoke:

> In any term we can posit a world, in the sense that we can treat the world *in terms of* it, seeing all as emanations, near or

far, of its light. Such reduction to a simplicity being technically reduction to a summarizing title or "God term," when we confront a simplicity we must forthwith ask ourselves what complexities are subsumed beneath it. [*Grammar of Motives*, p. 105]

I have taken "game" as my God term, and if I have in the heat of argument sometimes neglected the complexities subsumed beneath it, I am sure the novel's shrewd and combative admirers will not fail to notice.

I have contravened scholarly practice in citing recent paperback editions of secondary texts occasionally. I have done so simply because they are likely to be the editions most readers will own and thus most easily refer to.

Let me thank my good friend and former colleague, Professor Earl Miner, for careful reading of a typescript draft and for many valuable suggestions. I must also thank one of my excellent Sterne students, Miss Diane L. Clifford, who typed the manuscript, and my Research Assistant Miss Elena Barcia, who read the proof. And my wife, as proofreader, has once again saved me from several stupidities.

R. A. L.

CHAPTER ONE
Stoic Comedian and Victorian Jester

I

"In America," Dame Una Pope-Hennessy commented in reviewing Lewis Curtis's edition of the *Letters*, "Sterne has been taken seriously."[1] He certainly has. Instead of the Victorians' bavin-witted jester, we have seen a profound philosopher in— and of—the comic mode, a forerunner to the Stoic Comedians[2] of today's existential predicament. Modern students, while trying not to lose Sterne's sense of humor or their own, have again and again found his purpose serious and moral. Thirty years ago, W. B. C. Watkins cautioned that "one must not take him too seriously; yet one must take him seriously enough."[3] The second half of the *caveat* has borne the emphasis. B. H. Lehman, in a pioneering essay two years later, fixed Sterne's central work precisely: "*Tristram Shandy*, although it is a comedy, is a serious work, and it is serious throughout.... It is always ... a philosophic laughter."[4] Subsequent critics remind us repeatedly that "humor, too, is a serious matter."[5] For Sigurd Burckhardt,

[1] Dame Una Pope-Hennessy, "Laurence Sterne," *The Quarterly Review*, CCLXVI (January 1936), 87.

[2] The phrase is Hugh Kenner's, *Flaubert, Joyce and Beckett, The Stoic Comedians* (Boston, 1962).

[3] W. B. C. Watkins, "Yorick Revisited," *Perilous Balance* (Princeton, 1939), p. 123.

[4] B. H. Lehman, "Of Time, Personality, and the Author, A Study of *Tristram Shandy*: Comedy," in *Studies in the Comic*, University of California Publications in English, III, 2 (1941), 236.

[5] Dorothy Van Ghent, "On *Tristram Shandy*," *The English Novel: Form and Function* (New York, 1961), p. 95.

"Sterne's final joke is again and again that he is not joking."[6] Ben Reid, in an effort at summary and reappraisal, concludes that "by and large we have read Sterne badly because we have not read him with sufficient seriousness.[7] The wholehearted good humor of Sterne's jest," he continues, "is only the bright face of his comedy, not its whole soul." Of Sterne's didacticism, the French critic Henri Fluchère has recently written in his massive study: "Le didactisme avoué de l'oeuvre n'est qu'un masque plaisant (ou burlesque) qui dissimule un didactisme secret bien plus profond."[8] And the verbal play is no less serious than the didicaticism: "It is play, but play may be of a very serious kind."[9] Under this pressure toward seriousness, the scope of Sterne's thought, his characteristic grasp of the world, has seemed to expand enormously. Arthur J. Cash calls him "the most philosophic of novelists."[10] And John M. Stedmond sees *Tristram Shandy*'s comic mood as almost lyrically cosmic:

> The picture we get is of a creature whose destiny is radically beyond his control. Man, at the mercy of small chances, can be viewed as absurdly comic in his self-importance. He can also be seen as pathetic in his self-awareness. Sterne's comedy is a mingling of these two attitudes.[11]

Sterne has become a novelist of major statements, one whose "special sentimentalism, rightly understood, is a special manifestation of that endemic high seriousness which is the true

---

[6] Sigurd Burckhardt, "*Tristram Shandy*'s Law of Gravity," *ELH*, XXVIII (1961), 71.

[7] Ben Reid, "The Sad Hilarity of Sterne," *Virginia Quarterly Review*, XXXII (1956), 108, 109.

[8] Henri Fluchère, *Laurence Sterne, de l'homme à l'oeuvre* (Paris, 1961), pp. 240–241.

9. Robert A. Donovan, *The Shaping Vision: Imagination in the English Novel from Defoe to Dickens* (Ithaca, N.Y., 1966), p. 95.

[10] Arthur J. Cash, "The Sermon in *Tristram Shandy*," *ELH*, XXXI (1964), 416.

[11] John M. Stedmond, *The Comic Art of Laurence Sterne* (Toronto, 1967), p. 109.

ground swell of his art."¹² For many modern students Sterne aims at nothing less than "the heart of human reality."¹³

What kind of a philosopher has Sterne become? Cash has seen the Sterne of *A Sentimental Journey* (and, by implication, of everything else) as a radical Christian moralist whose "goals of life . . . were never to be found in man's emotional nature, and never in the pleasure principle":¹⁴ the Sterne of *The Sermons of Mr. Yorick*. But this view has hardly prevailed. Instead, commentators have concurred in Sterne as existentialist, even existential hero, and as philosopher of language. Here John Traugott's brilliant and pathfinding study¹⁵ has cast a long shadow. Man, in a world of, as Lehman says, "contingency incarnate," condemned to touch other men only through a language essentially elusive and undependable, strives ever to say what he means and mean what he says and can do neither, imprisoned in "a solipsistic view of the universe" where each of us rides his hobbyhorse "through his own private reality."¹⁶ What is such a man to do? Sterne's answer, for Traugott, is first to become aware of one's imprisonment in self by language, to become self-conscious about rhetoric, and second, to break out of the box of self by fellow-feeling, by sentiment. Sentiment, in a new way, stands again, as with the Victorians, at the heart of Sterne's genius.

¹² Reid, "Sad Hilarity," p. 115. Reid, half-expecting perhaps a Shandean laugh at so solemn a verdict, goes on to qualify it: "Perhaps we shall have to say that his seriousness was greater than he realized himself."

¹³ Jean-Jacques Mayoux, "Laurence Sterne" (original title: "Laurence Sterne parmi nous," in *Critique: Revue générale des publications françaises et étrangères*, XVIII, 177 [February 1962], 99–120), trans. John Traugott, reprinted in *Laurence Sterne: A Collection of Critical Essays*, ed. John Traugott (Englewood Cliffs, N.J., 1968), p. 113.

¹⁴ Cash, *Sterne's Comedy of Moral Sentiments: The Ethical Dimension of the "Journey"* (Pittsburgh, 1966), pp. 117–118.

¹⁵ John Traugott, *Tristram Shandy's World: Sterne's Philosophic Rhetoric* (Berkeley and Los Angeles, 1954).

¹⁶ Joan Joffe Hall, "The Hobbyhorsical World of *Tristram Shandy*," *MLQ*, XXIV (1963), 139.

Far from being a reproach to him, Sterne's sentimentalism is his greatest glory. His very special discovery of the limits of reason and the uses of sentimentalism marks him out the most original man of his century—whose lifeline we in our century gladly take —but still he shows his origins. In creativity and sentiment Sterne finds the answer to absurdity, though absurdity it is.[17]

Sentiment, in this orchestration, becomes the basis of society, and Sterne the first to see it. It figures as a Kierkegaardian leap of faith, the gesture (so like Toby's reaching out to his brother) upon which human fellowship depends. And Sterne, like Camus, becomes a visionary of the "Sentimental Absurd."[18]

Attractive as this conception has been to the modern temper, the conception of Sterne as philosopher of, novelist of, the creative process has appealed still more. As Martin Price has put it in a fine chapter ("Sterne: Art and Nature") in *To The Palace of Wisdom*:

> What matters for Sterne is the shift of attention from the embodied work to the energy of the artist, from the formed. . . to the forming, from the creation to the immanent creator.[19]

Dorothy Van Ghent wrote even more strongly. Creativity is Sterne's proper theme. "Sterne's project, like Proust's, was to analyze and represent in his novel the creative process. . . . In reading *Tristram Shandy*, we are never allowed to forget that

[17] Traugott, ed., Introduction to *Laurence Sterne: A Collection of Critical Essays*, p. 15. Other critics have echoed him, David Daiches for example: "Only the rush of affection can bridge the gulf that lies between individual consciousnesses. One might almost say that for Sterne one must be sentimental to escape from the prison of the private self." (*A Critical History of English Literature*, 2 vols. [London, 1960], 732–733.) And William Bowman Piper, in a recent study, expands sentimentality for Sterne to mean the whole of the emotive life. "It seems to be the essential cement for all human society, being capable by particular modifications of realizing itself as pity, love, fellow-feeling, loyalty, generosity, tolerance, and so forth." (*Laurence Sterne* [New York, 1965], p. 99.)

[18] See Ernest H. Lockridge, "A Vision of the Sentimental Absurd: Sterne and Camus," *Sewanee Review*, vol. LXXII (1964).

[19] Martin M. Price, *To the Palace of Wisdom* (New York, 1964), p. 331.

the activity of creation . . . *is itself the subject*."[20] The creative process here stands, clearly enough, for man's response, in its most ideal, most ordered form, to his absurd predicament. Sterne the novelist becomes man at work, trying to transcend the boundary conditions of his perception, to see around the edges of the universe and his place in it. His weapon has been not only sentiment but the classical weapon of words, undependable though they be. In a world where ideas do not really exist, words will have, as Burckhardt points out, a peculiar weight, will tend to become things, not what points but what is pointed at.[21] They may, in themselves, constitute the boundary conditions of perception. Sterne thus joins the modern philosophers of the limits of language, Cassirer, Langer, Whorf. For such, the manipulator of words becomes in a distinctively modern way the builder of a golden world created by man's wit. The poet displaces the scientist once again at the center of man's knowing.

The largest frame for Sterne as philosophic novelist, as someone highly serious for the modern world, has been supplied by Earl R. Wasserman.[22] He views Sterne as providing, in *Tristram Shandy*, the last, essentially "modern," chapter in the decay of Christendom, the stage of hobbyhorse and the radically private life.

> For during the eighteenth century the disintegration of cosmic orders widely felt as true was finally completed. In the Middle Ages and the Renaissance the literate had shared a constellation of synthesizing myths by means of which man could grasp relationships that gave significant pattern to otherwise discrete things

[20] Van Ghent, *The English Novel*, pp. 86, 87.
[21] Burckhardt, *"Tristram Shandy's* Law of Gravity." Juxtaposed with this view, put Cash's insistence that: "Sterne was an ethical 'realist.' He believed that the laws and obligations known to reason (sometimes also revealed beneficently by God) are the highest reality, not figments of the imagination or empty words." ("The Sermon in *Tristram Shandy,*" p. 407.)
[22] Earl R. Wasserman, *The Subtler Language* (Baltimore, 1959), pp. 169 ff.

and experiences. These systems transformed man and his world into a lexicon of symbols and integrated the symbols by meaningful cross-references. But by the end of the eighteenth century these communally accepted patterns had almost completely disappeared—each man now rode his own hobby-horse. No literate person before the eighteenth century could fail to grasp the full sense and implications of a comet, a circle, dew, a clash of the elements, the similarity of man and the world; for each of these was involved in a recognized network of images, significances, and values. But the news that Brother Bobby was dead had as many discrete meanings as the hobby-horses the auditors rode. And each rode a different one.

In Tristram's world, meaning had become a function of each person's private, subjective concerns, which alone remained as an interpretive organization. Everything is filtered for Walter Shandy through his various hypotheses; the implements, vocabulary, acts, and plans of warfare determine all significance for Uncle Toby; Tristram's hobby-horse is the recording of his life and opinions; Dr. Slop rides his obstetrics and his papistry; and nothing has meaning for Mrs. Shandy because she has no hobby-horse. What is more, in this completely individualistic world none of these private principles ever succeeds in organizing life, and chaos is forever breaking in.

Tristram Shandy lives, in this long view, as chronicler of chaos.

II

How seriously, indeed, we take Sterne. And how somber the modern Stoic Philosopher seems when set beside the Victorian Jester. We meet a different man. The attack everyone remembers is Thackeray's. But this was, though stimulating, an aberrant verdict.[23] Sir Walter Scott comes closer as prophet for the cen-

[23] "Just as Hazlitt had been the forerunner of a new sympathy and understanding in the approach of critics during the Romantic Age, Thackeray likewise set in motion a new train of critical comments from the Victorians. Though the pronouncements of Thackeray have not had the lasting effect that those of Hazlitt, Coleridge, and Scott have had, they neverthe-

tury's main charges: "If we consider Sterne's reputation as chiefly founded on *Tristram Shandy*, he must be regarded as liable to two severe charges;—those, namely, of indecency and affectation."[24] The modern commentator adroitly disposes of both. Indecency no longer bother us. As with Shakespeare, bawdry will always be philosophical, remind us of the inevitable limitations of the flesh. Affectation? It stands at the center of Sterne's genius. The self-conscious narrator, with all that he implies, constitutes his glory and place in literary history.[25] Yet the more one reads the Victorian dispraise of Sterne, the more one suspects grounds for dissatisfaction little related to affectation per se and even less to obscenity. The real issue clings as close to the hearts of the twentieth century as to the nineteenth. We praise him for the possessing, they damn him for the lacking of it: High Seriousness.

As egregious example of Victorian blindness, we could hardly do better than begin, not with Thackeray's fulminations, but with Walter Bagehot's review (1864) of Fitzgerald's *The Life of Laurence Sterne*.[26] He seems determined to make the modern critic wince. "Sterne's best things read best out of his books." *Tristram Shandy* "contains eccentric characters only." And in the novel there clearly is "indecency for indecency's sake." "Its style is fantastic, its method illogical and provoking." Worse still,

---

less have had to be reckoned with by subsequent critics, and their violently unfavorable tone has often tended to obscure the real attitude of the age toward Sterne." (Alan B. Howes, *Yorick and the Critics: Sterne's Reputation in England, 1760–1868* [New Haven, 1958], p. 143). Thackeray aimed, in his *Lectures on the English Humourists*, for a social as well as literary splash, and the damnation of Sterne, Howes continues, served his purposes, not the truth's.

[24] Sir Walter Scott, *Sir Walter Scott: On Novelists and Fiction*, ed. Ioan Williams (London, 1968), p. 72.

[25] See Wayne C. Booth, "The Self-Conscious Narrator in Comic Fiction before *Tristram Shandy*," *PMLA*, vol. LXVII (1952).

[26] It appears in volume II of Walter Bagehot's *Literary Studies* (ed. R. H. Hutton [London, 1916], pp. 282–325), along with a review of Theodore Taylor's life of Thackeray, under the title "Sterne and Thackeray."

Bagehot patronizes: "It is a great work of art, but of barbarous art. Its mirth is boisterous. It is *provincial*. It is redolent of an inferior society; of those who think crude animal spirits in themselves delightful,...who like disturbing transitions, blank pages, and tricks of style." Finally, the main charge: Sterne is brainless.

> He is a great author; certainly not because of great thoughts, for there is scarcely a sentence in his writings which can be called a thought; nor from sublime conceptions which enlarge the limits of our imagination, for he never leaves the sensuous,—but because of his wonderful sympathy with, and wonderful power of representing, simple human nature. . . . He is a great author because he felt acutely.

However outrageous Bagehot's response, the pattern of it stands clear. Farewell the philosophic mind. The novelist of incidental effect, working a single delicate, often abused capacity for feeling, Sterne becomes almost naïve. A comprehensive philosophic view of mankind gives way to the nice detail of pathetic genre-painting; coherent narrative to a typographical jester's tricks. The last person on earth from whom to expect high seriousness, Sterne is less damned than consigned forever to a minor mode. Inadequacy prevails, not sin. Bagehot, then, repudiates the inane jester, but accepts the man of feeling. High seriousness is specifically denied.

In the biographical sketch preceding his critical discussion, Bagehot offers an analogous observation about Sterne the man. He failed to sin greatly because he was not up to it. "Sterne was a pagan." His going into the Church was a mistake; it led him into an alien arena of moral demands. Not that he was not moral; he simply was not, could never be, religious. His sermons "are well expressed, vigorous, moral essays; but they are no more . . . they would be just as true if there was no religion at all." We should be clear: Bagehot does not condemn Sterne for immorality. He specifies a range, a limitation, of possible effect. Sterne came across, for Bagehot, as indecent and affected. But neither weakened his strength (the fine pathetic portraiture, the plain, amoral feeling) or strengthened his weakness (uniform absence of reflection if not altogether of mind, of any high seriousness whatsoever). Understanding Sterne so, Bagehot not unnaturally preferred *A Sentimental Journey* to *Tristram Shandy*. The Journey specializes in what he applauded. But what modern students now see nearly everywhere, he saw nowhere—more, he saw everywhere lacking—high seriousness.

It was not the pathos invitation but the jester invitation Thackeray[27] chose to accept:

> The humour of Swift and Rabelais, whom he pretended to succeed, poured from them as naturally as a song does from a bird; they lose no manly dignity with it, but laugh their hearty great laugh out of their broad chests as nature bade them. But this man—who can make you laugh, who can make you cry, too—never lets his reader alone, or will permit his audience repose: when you are quiet, he fancies he must rouse you, and turns over head and heels, or sidles up and whispers a nasty story. The man is a great jester, not a great humourist. He goes to work systematically and of cold blood; paints his face, puts on his ruff and motley clothes, and lays down his carpet and tumbles on it.

Again, the modern critical consensus reversed: no philosophy in Sterne's humor at all, no tragic underside. Thackeray, whatever motivated his condemnation, clearly condemns Sterne for his lack of high seriousness, his willingness to sacrifice anything for a laugh. He particularly resents *calculation*: "He is always looking in my face, watching his effect, uncertain whether I think him an imposter or not; posture-making, coaxing, and imploring me." The sublime emotions must lie altogether beyond such a clown's range. Calculation precludes them. Thackeray's resent-

[27] W. M. Thackeray, "Sterne and Goldsmith," in *The English Humourists of the Eighteenth Century* (New York, 1853), pp. 228–247.

ment, however well dramatized, is easy to understand. He resented being mocked for the easy manipulability of his feelings. More severely, he resented the implied insult to the feelings themselves. They were simply tools. Sterne used them selfishly, to draw attention to himself, not to them. Others have felt the same. Sir Leslie Stephen, for example: "He was resolved to attract notice at any price—by putting on cap and bells, and by the pruriency which stains his best work."[28] F. R. Leavis slaps at Sterne's "nasty trifling" with words in a note in *The Great Tradition*: Sterne fails to preserve that seriousness toward words and sex which the Tradition demands. Or we might cite a recent treatise on *Tragedy and Comedy*, Victorian in critical sophistication, by Walter Kerr: "I think there is only one kind of clown I cannot tolerate, and that is the kind who is himself uncommitted to what he is doing. A part of him is absent, listening, remembering, calculating."[29] The resentment felt at all periods by those who see Sterne retailing dirty jokes for profit is curiously alike. Sterne will not take sex seriously. Victorians would have him denounce it, Moderns applaud, at least philosophize it. By laughing at it, Sterne displeased both. Aware of his self-exploitation too, he refused to fuss over it either. So to Kitty Fourmantel: "P. S. There is a fine print going to be done of me— so I shall make the most of myself, & sell both inside & out." And to Stephen Croft, with a Shakespearean practicality: "One half of the town abuse my book as bitterly, as the other half cry it up to the skies—the best is, they abuse and buy it."[30]

For Thackeray, then, prurience and affectation formed part of a larger, more fundamental objection—Sterne's essential frivolity. Everything was for sale, everything available for effect. Nothing was serious. Sterne was indeed a pagan. Thackeray cer-

---

[28] Sir Leslie Stephen, *English Literature and Society in the Eighteenth Century* (London, 1940), p. 201.

[29] Walter Kerr, *Tragedy and Comedy* (New York, 1967), pp. 14–15.

[30] Laurence Sterne, *Letters of Laurence Sterne*, ed. Lewis P. Curtis (Oxford, 1935), pp. 105, 129.

tainly could conceive of serious, reflective comedy. In the lecture immediately after that on Sterne ("Charity and Humour"), he describes a "humorous writer" almost indistinguishable from the modern profile of Sterne the Stoic Comedian.

> Besides contributing to our stock of happiness, to our harmless laughter and amusement, to our scorn for falsehood and pretension, to our righteous hatred of hypocrisy, to our education in the perception of truth, our love of honesty, our knowledge of life, and shrewd guidance through the world, have not our humourous writers, our gay and kind week-day preachers, done much in support of . . . the cause of love and charity, the cause of the poor, the weak, and the unhappy; the sweet mission of love and tenderness, and peace and goodwill towards men? That same theme which is urged upon you by the eloquence and example of good men to whom you are delighted listeners on Sabbath-days, is taught in his way and according to his power by the humorous writer, the commentator on every-day life and manners.
>
> A literary man of the humoristic turn is pretty sure to be of a philanthropic nature, to have a great sensibility, to be easily moved to pain or pleasure, keenly to appreciate the varieties of temper of people round about him, and sympathise in their laughter, love, amusement, tears.

Precisely this pattern, he makes clear by his strategy of contrasting juxtaposition in the two lectures, Sterne failed to fit.

The gravamen of the Victorian charge has recurred occasionally since. Governor Cross thought Sterne "incapable of high seriousness," a "humourist pure and simple." Cyril Connolly, in a popular essay in the *Atlantic Monthly*[31] saw Sterne as "not a man of deep feelings." And Saintsbury, too, saw him as a man of the middle effect:

> Sterne has no doubt in a very eminent degree the sense of contrast, which all the best critics admit to be the root of humour—

---

[31] Cyril Connolly, "Sterne and Swift," vol. CLXXV (June, 1945).

the note of the humourist. But he has it partially, occasionally, and, I should even go as far as to say, not *greatly*. . . . It is scarcely too much to say that his ostentatious preference for the *bagatelle* was a real and not in the least affected fact. . . . His forte is the foible; his *cheval de bataille*, the hobby-horse. If you want to soar into the heights or plunge into the depths of humour, Sterne is not for you.[32]

Saintsbury is shrewder on Sterne as actor:

It was an age of great actors: and I fancy—though perhaps because I am better able to judge it in his case than in the other— that Sterne was as great an actor in one way as his friend Garrick was in most others. [P. 165]

But if he was an actor rather than a creator, then we can give him the quality of greatness freely, for so great an actor is nowhere to be found in literature. [P. 193]

Even Lehman:

In some senses of the word Laurence Sterne was, of course, not a philosopher. He had little or no feeling for great ideas, great ways of life, or for great spirits dedicated to such ways of life, inspired by such ideas.[33]

But the scholar who has most nearly preserved the Victorian conception of Sterne is, paradoxically, Ernest N. Dilworth. Dilworth, like Thackeray, finds Sterne not a great humorist but a great jester, though, most unlike Thackeray, he applauds the lack of high seriousness. Sterne's very absence of moral purpose is, for him, morally corrective:

The man who looks morally down his nose at Sterne is invited, before he passes judgment, to explore the cesspool of his own self-interest. The egotistical affectations of Sterne were as harmless and open as the grimaces of a clown; he changed costume

---

[32] George Saintsbury, *Prefaces and Essays* (London, 1933), pp. 148–149.
[33] Lehman, "Of Time, Personality, and the Author," p. 236.

before the eyes of his audience; he frankly enjoyed himself as the good Lord made him, and the Lord had not made him serious. Frivolity was his mainspring.[34]

The two attitudes combine oddly. Sterne's pure jesting becomes itself a serious matter. No stronger example comes to mind of the urge to put Sterne's jesting to use, to moralize his song.[35]

III

Through the agency of Victorian demurrer, we have dichotomized the commentary on Sterne in the last century and a half. For the one side Sterne, pathetic beauty excepted, plays venial jester. For the other, he reenacts existential philosopher, confronting absurdity with a jest but preoccupied, finally, with the most serious problems, the most fundamental issues. The confronting camps surprise by a major agreement: for both, the issue is Sterne's seriousness. This divides them. The division gives pause. Even Milton has not been subjected to such precipitous reëvaluation, such divergent appreciation. Sterne's effort to engender both responses, however, suggests searching for a common ground. Each side has extracted, has pleaded only to what fits its theory. The Victorians covered their tracks less well, but the reader of a thesis like Traugott's, brilliant as it is, will hold both camps culpable. Common ground cannot come, it seems clear, with "seriousness" defined as it is. Sterne either will possess it or will not. We must discard one half of the historical response either way. A more promising approach might work at redefining "seriousness." For this purpose, it is no longer possible (as we shall see more fully in the last chapter) to think of life and work as a single body.

[34] Ernest N. Dilworth, *The Unsentimental Journey of Laurence Sterne* (New York, 1948), p. 80.

[35] Dilworth plays here for Victorians the same role of loyal opposition with agreement in principle that Cash has played for the Moderns.

Wayne Booth commented, in his review of Dilworth's essay, that "he fails, like most of Sterne's critics, to separate the man and the works sufficiently to allow for artistic considerations."[36] And the Victorians, too, Thackeray especially, have felt the whip for confusing man and work. In fact, this happened from the beginning. "There is no time during the entire period from 1760 to 1868 when biographical considerations do not have an important influence upon the criticism of Sterne."[37] And it has continued, from A. De Froe's forlorn Freudianism[38] to Fluchère. However necessary it may be to separate the two, students of Sterne have always found it hard. So Lodwick Hartley, summarizing the criticism: "It is, of course, possible to say that Sterne wrote only one book and that this book includes everything that he wrote: sermons, letters, journals, novels."[39] Although a Coleridge might occasionally praise *Tristram Shandy* and damn *A Sentimental Journey*, or a Hazlitt reverse the preference, most readers have felt that all was somehow of a piece. The letters were full of artifice, of posing, like the life, like everything else. At the same time, and from the beginning of Sterne's career,[40] no one could say what the piece really was. About the relation of work to life, the most diverse opinions stepped forward. Almost from the start, he was extensively read in extract, in collections of "beauties." Sterne the man was often appraised from hearsay. On the one hand, man and work belonged together; on the other, they began to fall apart.[41] Facile

[36] Booth, review of *The Unsentimental Journey of Laurence Sterne*, *MP*, XLVI (1949), 280–282.

[37] Howes, *Yorick and the Critics*, p. 174.

[38] A. De Froe, *Laurence Sterne and His Novels Studied in the Light of Modern Psychology* (Groningen, 1925).

[39] Lodwick Hartley, *Laurence Sterne in the Twentieth Century* (Chapel Hill, N.C., 1966), p. 35.

[40] Howes, *Yorick and the Critics*, p. 21.

[41] "Finally, the presence of so many diverse elements in Sterne often gave rise to misinterpretations of his work, for few readers, during his own time or later, saw the interrelationship of the different parts. Though the presence of satire, humor, and pathos in a single work helped to account

generalization has been the curse of Sterne criticism from the beginning. Evidence has been picked like flowers in a field, biography and fiction part of the same bouquet. Useful as it may be for some purposes, such eclecticism would be fatal for ours. We need a hard body of evidence, a literary form. This can only be *Tristram Shandy*. Such a restriction does not mean that general conclusions about the whole of Sterne's life and work cannot be drawn, but simply that they do not offer a promising beginning. If we are to isolate the peculiar configuration of Sterne's seriousness, we must define the seriousness of his major work.

IV

Sterne himself, a few months before his death, in returning thanks to Dr. John Eustace for praise of *Shandy*, remarked on its invitation to different interpretations:

> Your walking stick is in no sense more *shandaic* than in that of its having *more handles than one*—The parallel breaks only in this, that in using the stick, every one will take the handle which suits his convenience. In *Tristram Shandy*, the handle is taken which suits their [the readers'] passions, their ignorance or sensibility.[42]

We can, at this later date, see a pattern in the handles readers have chosen to grasp. Sterne's own time grasped the Tristram handle. The cleverness, the wit, the freakishness of the novel struck them. They relished its learned wit as never since. The nineteenth century (Hazlitt more than anyone else signals the change) chose the Toby handle. Again and again the good Uncle reaps the praise. All Sterne's redeeming pathos and humor found in him their symbol, exemplum, and defender. The twentieth century prefers to think that, seeing the novel whole for the

---

for the initial success of *Tristram Shandy*, few critics could appreciate all three elements equally, and even fewer found them appropriately joined" (*ibid.*, p. 176).

[42] Sterne, *Letters*, p. 411.

first time, we grasp all the handles at once. In some ways this is true, but without belittling the excellent commentary of the last twenty years, have we too not grasped a single handle, the one that suits our passions, our ignorance, or our sensibility? Do we not look increasingly like Walter Shandy? The Victorians, tuned for the pathos, could not get enough of Le Fever's death; the Moderns, obsessed with the prison of the self, all cite the report of Bobby's. Equally strong selection works in both. Are we really so far from the Victorians? We find what they sought in vain. The pattern of expectation seems much the same.

Tristram Shandy sets a series of traps for its readers and we have fallen into one of them. We now expand that one, render it coexistent with the novel as a whole. The history of the novel's glosses indicates a finite number of traps. So does its structure. Tristram sets the first, Toby the second. Walter stands for a third, and possibly Yorick for a different kind of fourth, a trap into which, historically, criticism has not yet fully tumbled. Any reading of the novel should offer a map through the minefield. It is tempting to see, in the modern critical consensus, just such a map. We look at each of the characters imprisoned in himself yet reaching out through real and symbolic gesture, and we see a map of the absurd universe, the hobbies, the traps and the pathetic, comic glories of man.

> It is man's nature to strive after inaccessible goals, and, in this striving, he is a comic figure: the clown pushing a peanut with his nose across a continent. But without this drive on the one hand, leading to small temporary accomplishments, and the ever receding horizon of attainment on the other, there would be no such thing as human life. Paradoxically, if man were ever able to achieve final answers, he would have moved himself to another plane of existence, he would no longer be "human" in our understanding of the term.[43]

[43] Stedmond, *Comic Art*, p. 131.

So we see modern man's pathetic, comic, yet finally sometimes (wry grin) magnificent efforts to cope with ineluctable circumstance. But surely this tendency to feel sorry for ourselves, to admire ourselves for sticking it out in an absurd universe, is precisely one of the attitudes that *Tristram Shandy* was written to mock. Sterne unhappily did not live to see the solemn self-pity that accompanies modern exegesis of our existential predicament. Had he seen, he certainly would not have spared. For his eye watched above all for sentimentality, for our penchant to extract pleasure from the bravest and the bitterest reflections. And he was the first to surprise such temptation in himself. So he writes to John Hall-Stevenson, in June of 1761:

> Tomorrow morning, (if Heaven permit) I begin the fifth volume of Shandy—I care not a curse for the critics—I'll load my vehicle with what goods *he* sends me, and they may take 'em off my hands, or let them alone—I am very valourous—and 'tis in proportion as we retire from the world and see it in its true dimensions, that we despise it—no bad rant![44]

Such readiness to see himself a self-satisfying actor casts suspicion on any view of Sterne as enduring, or preaching endurance in *Tristram Shandy*. He has had miseries and has not, he says in the same letter to Stevenson, managed them wisely. But "God, for my consolation . . . poured forth the spirit of Shandeism into me, which will not suffer me to think two moments upon any grave subject." The spirit of Shandeism *works*. Tristram does not endure. He triumphs. And Sterne with him.

The trouble with comedy is that no one will leave it alone. The joke must always be more than a joke. Pleasure is never enough. We must milk it for wisdom. Yet to do so denies comedy its domain and its power. The Victorians in their way and we in ours have denied it for *Tristram Shandy* because to come to terms with pleasure seems to imply an end to significance and,

[44] Sterne, *Letters*, pp. 139–140.

worse still, to discussion. Modern critics curtsy only to shy away. So Elizabeth Drew, in a popular history of the novel, tells us first that Sterne was "unique in his own day and unlike any other major novelist since in making no pretensions to be doing anything but enjoy himself and entertain his readers." Then, drawing back from this lonely eminence a few pages later, she applies to *Tristram Shandy* Sterne's avowed purpose in *A Sentimental Journey*: "To teach us to love the world and our fellow creatures better than we do."[45] To admit comedy's dedication to the pleasure-principle consigns Sterne to the frivolous pastures of the bagatelle. The theoretical answer to this conundrum I do not pretend to know. But for Sterne it seems clear. We must find a more adequate definition of Sterne's seriousness. Such a one must explain Sterne's kind of comedy without reducing it to frivolity on the one hand or philosophizing it into sobriety on the other. The principal agency of critical confusion here has been the assumption—by no means tacit but almost universal—that *Tristram Shandy* is an experimental novel. Thus placed against the alien background of modern fictional expectation, it has been made to choose one of two dichotomous paths. Both apply to the novel an essentially forward reference. It must be serious like Thackeray or it must be serious like Camus. Our first business must be to remove it from this alien ground and reestablish it in the proper tradition, the older tradition of classical, rhetorical, narrative forms. From that older tradition flows the definition of man and society, the kind of seriousness and the kind of comedy *Tristram Shandy* chooses to imitate.

[45] Elizabeth Drew, *The Novel: A Modern Guide to Fifteen English Masterpieces* (New York, 1963), pp. 75, 78.

CHAPTER TWO
Apocryphal Narrative
and Rhetorical Man

I

At one point in the midst of Volume I, Tristram takes up his favorite Adversarius, the inattentive Madam, for a failure to read closely. He then turns to us, parenthetically, with this:

'Tis to rebuke a vicious taste which has crept into thousands besides herself,—of reading straight forwards, more in quest of the adventures, than of the deep erudition and knowledge which a book of this cast, if read over as it should be, would infallibly impart with them.—The mind should be accustomed to make wise reflections, and draw curious conclusions as it goes along.[1]

And after a detour through the Younger Pliny and the Seven Champions of England, he picks up the thread again.

It is a terrible misfortune for this same book of mine, but more so to the Republick of Letters;—so that my own is quite swallowed up in the consideration of it,—that this self-same vile pruriency for fresh adventures in all things, has got so strongly into our habit and humours,—and so wholly intent are we upon satisfying the impatience of our concupiscence that way,—that nothing but the gross and more carnal parts of a composition will go down:—The subtle hints and sly communications of science fly

---

[1] Laurence Sterne, *The Life and Opinions of Tristram Shandy, Gentleman*, ed. James A. Work (New York, 1940), I, xx, 56. All subsequent citations are taken from this edition.

off, like spirits, upwards;—the heavy moral escapes downwards; and both the one and the other are as much lost to the world, as if they were still left in the bottom of the ink-horn.

The excursus concludes with a pious thought that male readers, as well as female, "be taught to think as well as read." In question here stands the novelistic expectation, the desire to follow story as reality, not as story. Tristram reasserts the claim of an older reader-writer relationship that, as Fielding or later Trollope sometimes does, acknowledges illusion and invites the reader to reflection rather than entrancement. The vile pruriency for fresh adventure appears the new thing to Tristram, the reflective pattern, the older. Modern criticism has reversed the order. Precursor to the modern novel or mocker of the traditional, *Tristram Shandy* in either case measures itself against a novelistic norm. Such reference makes it, for us, seem at once newer than it was and much different, much, as we shall see, more serious. The malign influence of so peculiarly ahistorical a standard has operated, of course, on all early fiction, especially Renaissance fiction, where the inane hunt for the first novel often begins. We comb the history of fiction for forerunners of the novel, much as the Romans considered all previous history the youth of Rome. But it has worked especially strongly against *Tristram Shandy*, making us see it as a diabolically clever and diabolically philosophic process-novel, one that aims at much greater realism, a much more accurate psychological space and time, than fiction had up to that point attained.[2]

Such an expectation allows the book a seriousness Sterne was concerned to prohibit. For his "book apocryphal" does not allow us to rest in any single genre, certainly not in any realistic one,

[2] So B. H. Lehman writes: "To see what Sterne's achievement really was, is I believe only in these last years possible, in a mind made aware by *The Magic Mountain*, *Ulysses*, and *The Remembrance of Things Past*." ("Of Time, Personality, and the Author, A Study of *Tristram Shandy*: Comedy," in *Studies in the Comic*, University of California Publications in English, III, 2 [1941], 234.)

long enough for us to accept its definition of reality unreservedly. He builds up, rather, a pattern of overlapping genres that are calculated to deny us a single consistent set of rules, definition of reality, and the seriousness that such a definition permits. His narrative, by design, is no one thing.

Tristram Shandy springs up as everyone says, and none more than its narrator, *sui generis*. But if we ask what it is like, the novel, eighteenth century or twentieth century, would hardly occur to us first. One of the things Tristram calls it is a history.

> For which cause, right glad I am, that I have begun the history of myself in the way I have done; and that I am able to go on tracing every thing in it, as Horace says, *ab Ovo*. [I, iv, 7]

History, to Sterne, offered a far different narrative expectation than to us. He would have conceived it as Herodotus and Thucydides between them established it for the Latin historians; as Herodotean combination of event, comment on event, and illustrative digression, or as a Thucydidean alternation of narrative and rhetorical debate. In both he would have found those "subtle lines and sly communications" he sees as vanishing from narrative in his own time. Both offer a considerably more complex conception of "event" than the modern historian would permit. Both furnish narrative comment and comment on the narrative, background, reference to hearer's opinion, truly Shandean motive-mongering. And both include a great deal of rhetoric, of formal speechifying in the high style. Historical writing to the close of the Renaissance is saturated with rhetoric and the historical pattern was borrowed for other kinds of narrative as well. The Hellenistic romances reflect it almost invariably: descriptive passage—event—elaborate rhetorical encounter, *da capo*. The rhetoric, often called ornamental, is really quite the reverse, comes at the deepest moments, not the superficial.

In the ancient world, at the point of most intense penetration into the inner life, in the monologues we have been considering, we find not psychology but rhetoric, and it is rhetoric which dominates the monologue of characterization in all Western literature, from the Greeks to the Renaissance, not excluding the great monologues in Chaucerian narrative and Shakespearean drama.[3]

Uncle Toby recalls this propensity in commenting on the hot spot in Trim's love story: "—And then, thou clapped'st it to thy lips, *Trim*, said my uncle *Toby*—and madest a speech." (VIII, xxiii, 575). The great speeches in Thucydides, Pericles' Funeral Oration, the Melian debate, establish a counterpoint with event; high style against low; professed motive against real; exposition against mimesis to follow. The narrative technique does not change in Livy, Tacitus, Suetonius, even in Shakespeare's history plays. And in *Tristram Shandy* we have Trim's reading of the Sermon, Bobby's death and its *lamentatio*, the great debate on name-changing into which the hot chestnut so precipitately drops. This alternation of narrative and rhetorical occasion creates highly dramatic, highly self-conscious history, factual narrative presented with fictional force. And the rhetorical exchanges create what Tristram repeatedly thinks of, on the classical model, as drama. The narrative interludes provide an inviting opportunity for the narrator to comment, become drama critic. The reader passes, in *Tristram Shandy* as in Thucydides or Livy, to connoisseurship not only of motive but of language. He steps, not closer to the tale, but farther from it. As with the historians, he is continually asked to judge. The narrator too:

> Let that be as it may, as my purpose is to do exact justice to every creature brought upon the stage of this dramatic work. [I, x, 18]

And Tristram argues continually for the illustrative digression of classical narrative, the interpolated epyllion travestied by the tale of Slawkenbergius. The paradigm of narrative procedure in

[3] Robert Scholes and Robert Kellogg, *The Nature of Narrative* (New York, 1966), p. 185.

I, xiv, might do unchanged for Herodotus. It does not create, however, realistic fiction, traditional or innovative. It deliberately denies us the suspension of disbelief that realism, however indirect, artfully contrived, depends on. It continually calls our attention to narrative artifice, stylistic surface, the reader's status as reader (or listener). The narrative of *Tristram Shandy* thus departs not from fictional models but, through Rabelais, from ones far older. And Tristram, like Rabelais, *plays* with the older models. The forms of classical historical narrative constitute his game.

A history, *Tristram Shandy* is also an autobiography/biography of the older epideictic type, illustrative incidents arranged in thematic rather than chronological pattern. But here too a private, not a public life finds voice. In fact, if for sanctity we substitute idiosyncrasy, cannot we begin to see something like a saint's life, Sterne's sanctification of the private life? A central crucial incident for Tristram cuts off the old life and starts the new; true motive opens like a flower to a zeal for going *ad fontes*; childhood is racked for prophetic omen; the weight of received learning dips in the scale with naïve feeling, fresh faith. But on top of this older biographical pattern Sterne has superposed the new. *Tristram Shandy* presents itself as incredibly, indeed ludicrously, zealous for detailed information. Tristram's life and times are to be presented with microscopic fidelity. What to make of it all Tristram, like the modern biographer, leaves up to us. And Tristram too fears to generalize. The two conflicting biographical patterns once again deny us a reference point, a firm footing. Both old and new mode of biography has each its kind of seriousness. But the two together in *Tristram Shandy* leave us bewildered. Which kind of truth, of seriousness are we to seek? Not *what* but *how* are we to believe? History and biography/ autobiography, *Tristram Shandy* stands as close to a third type, the rhetorical sampler. It is full of rhetorical instance. The three divisions of rhetoric are illustrated: forensic, deliberative, epideictic. Invention, arrangement, style, memory, especially delivery are constantly subjects of conversation. It not only uses the tropes and schemes, it talks about using them, and wishes to use them correctly ("if there be no catechesis in the wish"). As its two opposing character types it offers the Naturally Eloquent and the Naturally Dumb Man. It discusses the uses of oratory, and the need, when need there be, to move beyond it. It argues, describes, feels, explains, and—had the Widow Wadman not so justly bored Sterne—it would have made love. It develops a *controversia* on breeching the child. It rings changes on the three styles. It perpetually concerns itself with rhetorical as well as social decorum. Tristram continually puts hypothetical cases, extrapolates both sides of a disputation. *Tristram Shandy*, in fact, smells of the lamp. It is schoolbook and schoolboy comedy, like Nashe's *Unfortunate Traveller* or Lyly's *Euphues*, or like Lucian's *True History*. And, as with all these, criticism errs when it seeks narrative continuity, thematic development, depth of character—or a deliberate contravention of any of these fictional requirements. Breadth of illustration, ironic juxtaposition are to be sought much rather. And celebration of the power of oratory. Tristram, for example, reenacts Tacitus's ironic Afer (in the *Dialogue on Oratory*), grave amidst the decay of eloquence.

> It is a singular stroke of eloquence (at least it was so, when eloquence flourished at *Athens* and *Rome*, and would be so now, did orators wear mantles). . . . All of which plainly shews, may it please your worships . . . the decay of eloquence. [III, xiv, 185]

It celebrates speaking *extempore* as well as from a prepared text—the contrast, for Tristram, between writing full and writing fasting (VI, xvii, 436). He tells us compulsively that he speaks off the top of his head, trusting to God, or his pen, for what comes after. Another of *Tristram Shandy's* basic contrasts, between the general and the particular, works in a rhetorical ground. Tristram is always moving, and telling us that he is moving, from the general thesis to the particular: "But mine, indeed, is a particular case." And he loves to catalogue his responses into formal rhetorical occasions, as with the chapter of THINGS:

> In less than five minutes I shall have thrown my pen into the fire, and the little drop of thick ink which is left remaining at the bottom of my ink-horn, after it—I have but half a score things to do in the time—I have a thing to name—a thing to lament—a thing to hope—a thing to promise, and a thing to threaten—I have a thing to suppose—a thing to declare—a thing to conceal—a thing to chuse, a thing to pray for.—[IV, xxxii, 336]

Words, of course, are "things" in the rhetorical display-books just as they are in *Tristram Shandy*. Tristram treats them, often, as having actual weight. The *sententia* is a commodity imported into England (V, xii, 368–369). Remarks, like chestnuts, are dropped. Words also become places, Walter finding for example, that the Northwest passage to the intellectual world lies through the auxiliary verbs (V, xlii, 404).

"Writing," Tristram tells us, "when properly managed, (as you may be sure I think mine is) is but a different name for conversation...." And throughout he betrays the classical preference for the spoken over the written word. He lays down a clear middle style and makes it a symbol as well as a subtle vehicle for dialectic. Against this work the different styles of formally prepared, written speech. The written word plays with, against, the spoken. Thus Tristram manages to build into his discourse the ancient quarrel between the method of philosophy and the method of rhetoric; to write a manual of conversation, of dialectic, as well as oratory. His is to be a *complete book* of verbal disputation.

Rhetorical manuals are creatures of the marketplace. So with *Tristram Shandy*. Its Virgin Dedication (I, viii, and ix, 15 ff.) is put up for sale. Its sentimental passages are easily detachable for separate bouquets. Tristram's eye is always, like the Sophists', on the audience, and willing to play to it. He calls attention to his struggles as author, volumes unsold, volumes unwritten. He seems, as he depicts himself from publication to publication, to be *following* a market as much as creating one.

Tristram Shandy as rhetorical pattern-book works, even more sharply than as history or biography, to undermine the mimetic seriousness of realistic fiction. Once we become connoisseurs of language, we can no longer feel deeply about character or event. Nothing is real. All is example, and we feel it as example, as pretext. We are being taught and told that we are being taught. So too it is with still another classical genre that lurks behind Tristram's tale, the *speculum principis*. *Tristram Shandy* realizes a tristful *paideia* to be sure, a mockery of how the thing should go. But the book includes many of the elements the mirror of a perfect prince stressed. It starts punningly *ab ovo*. It dwells, as did Quintilian, Castiglione, Elyot's *Governor*, on the influence of very early youth. (The whole tradition in this respect is as Freudian as *Tristram Shandy*.) It considers the dangers of precocity, ending with Yorick's defense of the great Lipsius, "who composed a work the day he was born." (Toby writes the *finis* here: "—They should have wiped it up.") The relation of the good man and the good orator, a staple concern of the type, is allegorized clearly enough in *Tristram Shandy* by the relation of Walter and Toby Shandy. The mock-learning muddles out an imitation of the endless disputes over ideal curriculum in the genre. Here, of course, Sterne had Rabelais's example, *Gargantua and Pantagruel* being, among other things, a parody of the humanistic as well as medieval curriculum. The continual fuss about social decorum sports with the endless debates on manners, from the *Cyropaedia* onward. And the stress on conversation as educational finds counterpart in the *Courtier* and the *Republic* to which that treatise looked back. Walter writes a formal *Tristrapaedia* obviously intended to contrast ironically with the real one life has written and with which Tristram himself is playing games. He includes a pertinent, very funny conversation (VI, v, 415) on the perfect Governor. Toby and the fly are "to serve for parents and governors instead of a whole volume" (II, xii, 114). The sentimental *tableaux vivants* present themselves as dialectic, the real *paideia*, shooting directly to the heart. Read its sentimental half only and the book charts out nicely as sentimental *speculum*. Read the whole and, as we shall see, it comes near to being a mirror for the private life. We have our choice: serious mirror, comic mirror, some union of the two. Once again the choices deny us a simple point of view and the seriousness that goes with it.

In the later volumes, *Tristram Shandy* begins to echo the classical travel book. The travel metaphor occurs early: the landscape of the mind. And set piece description comes early too. Tristram, for example, in II, ix, 105, asks "Pray, Sir, let me interest you a moment in this description." Obadiah and Dr. Slop then collide. Punning on narrative geography, Tristram calls "plain stories" stories that take place on a plain (VII, xliii, 536). The past five volumes, reviewed at the beginning of six, become a countryside: "let us just look back upon the country we have pass'd through" (p. 408). Not until he goes on his travels do we get the travel book imitation direct. Here too the pattern is reductive. Tristram describes not the public monuments but, like a romantic Pausanias, the private moments. And the strange adventures, here, become a Fieldingesque reduction to the familiar of adventures that Hellenistic romance spoofs, that Voltaire parodies in *Zadig*.

Such comparisons as these only touch the surface of Sterne's game with the patterns of classical prose but should make the point clear. Sterne's innovations do not stand within the range of expectation realistic fiction holds out. He did not extend the domain of the novel. Much rather, he appropriated its subject for an elaborate game with classical narrative patterns. These are rhetorical, nonmimetic, nonrealistic. They would not surprise Sterne's audience. What did? What was new? Surely it was just this application of the older narrative techniques to the new *subject* of realistic narrative, the private life. For they fit, none of them, the *object* they are used to describe, the Shandy family, the pattern of unassertive private, retired obscurity. They are all types from the public life, each describing in its own way a public self, a *hypocrisis*, a stylized, acted version of the personality. Sterne brings the whole weight of this tradition into the private life. Here I think is the radical discontinuity of the book, here the comic incongruity. All the nonnovelistic techniques are used for a novelistic purpose. The means of chronicling Athens and Rome now chronicle Shandy Hall. Tristram's embarrassment is not, as has been suggested, that he is asked to talk politely about impolite subjects. It is that he must devise a mimesis of family life with materials devised to describe a life quite different and precisely mismatched for the job in hand. He does the best he can. Sterne's victory, through him, is to transfer the public world and public self into the domain of private life. By forcing Tristram to play the classical narrator, to use rhetorical techniques, in describing the private life, he makes us accept his conception of the private life as essentially rhetorical, dramatic, acted—full of ceremony. We are thus once again trapped between two expectations, the seriousness of the public life (the Victorian expectation) and the seriousness of the private (the modern expectation). Because we hardly know which world we are in, public or private, we cannot become fully serious about either. And our ambivalence lasts the whole book through.

If Sterne enters the house of mimetic fiction, then, he comes in very much by the back door. He wrote, not the first experimental novel but the last classical narrative. He used the techniques that, until Rabelais, had set forth the public world to set forth a radically private one. If we are now prepared to view the private world as *essentially* dramatic, ironically imprisoned in rhetoric, unalterably self-conscious, forever despoiled of its imaginative virginity, then we can think of Sterne as a realist. But this does not prove him one. It suggests much rather that we have returned to an older conception of reality, to the world of classical rhetorical theory, a world centered in drama and the word. We see Sterne as a realist because we have changed our conception of reality.

Sterne thus creates, for us, a work of mimetic fiction and a rhetorical treatise at the same time, novel and nonnovel. *Sui generis* indeed. And, although we shall for stylistic ease continue to call it a novel, might a more precise term be found? What fits the peculiar configuration we have just outlined, a collation of classical narrative types, rhetorical and nonmimetic, applied to the description of private life, used for pleasure? And if we add that the characters of this private life are themselves aware of the forms and pattern their behavior by them? And that the whole aims to sell, to please? Tristram calls his book "an entertainment" (II, ii, 84). But the sense of the English word is now too frivolous and too general, prejudices the case. What of its Latin counterpart *ludus*? The Latin preserves a fuller range of meanings: one that pulls together the public and the private domains; public spectacle or game, stage-playing, joking, private amusement. It can cover Sterne's game, Tristram's narrower narrative game, Toby's military one, Walter's philosophic ones. Above all, it reflects what all share, keep in common with the classical narrative patterns: all are self-conscious about language and literary form, making of language a *ludus*, a knowing public display of rhetoric, a game. Thus the word for the *form* of the book can point to the *theme* of the book as well, the rhetorical definition of man.

II

The premises of realistic fiction are not only scientific but Platonic. A reality exists beyond words which words can point to; a self (a soul for Plato) to which verbal imitation can draw ever closer. Plato would not have accepted this, poetry and rhetoric for him being two similar kinds of lying. The realistic novel departs from his orchestration of reality nevertheless. It conceives words as essentially neutral, translucent if not transparent: word points to event and in event lies reality. It moves toward a denotative, reportorial prose just as, with the prose of Defoe, it departed from one. Such a picture, such a caricature, holds true as counterstatement to the ground rules of rhetorical narrative. This latter from the beginning proceeded on Sophistic assumptions about man and society.[4]

The volumes that analyze the influence of rhetorical theory on Western literature fall, nowadays, as thick as snowflakes in Siberia. But they preoccupy themselves with fine detail, naming the tropes as they march by, counting off the seven battalions of the classical oration. No one, as Father Ong recently pointed out,[5] has concerned himself with the philosophical implications of rhetorical theory, with its definition of man. What did it think, and what did it train, man to be? Let us review such elements of rhetorical man as bear on our purpose.

The rhetorical orchestration of man views him as an incorrig-

---

[4] Criticism's quarrel with the older kind of narrative has come, in fact, from the persistent Platonism of literary theory. The endless charges of inaccuracy and rhetorical artificiality brought against the classical way of writing history, of overdecoration brought against Hellenistic romance and its progeny (Sidney's *Arcadia*, for example) stem from a conception of the word alien to the documents considered.

[5] "The effects of the academic cultivation of rhetoric and dialectic upon the psychological structures of pretechnical man have never been fully described and seldom even adverted to." (Walter J. Ong, S.J., *The Presence of the Word* [New Haven, 1967], p. 215.) Kenneth Burke would seem an obvious exception to this sound generalization.

ible roleplayer. He is *essentially* a speaker of lines. No Platonic self exists. The implication of rhetorical training, of the traditional concern with *ethos* (the character of the speaker) and *pathos* (the feelings of the audience) is identity largely as dramatic creation, a function of situation, of needful role and needful audience. The elaboration of the *topoi*, the reduction of situation to formula, ends (as with the Gestalt psychologists) by rendering situation essentially formulaic. The dramatic metaphor reigns supreme for society as well. All the world indeed becomes a stage. Life moves from scene to scene without cinematic dissolves. And the scenes, though the alternation may be sudden, inconsistent, unchronological (all these happen in *Tristram Shandy*) remain essentially discrete. So do human attitudes. To strike a pose is easy, fixed. The difficulty, as Tristram tells us, is moving from one to the other: "Attitudes are nothing, madam,—'tis the transition from one attitude to another ... which is all in all" (IV, vi, 276–277).

The rhetorical view of man grows violently reductive of human motive. If you practice pleading others' cases for your own profit, you end up implying, by your own life style, two kinds of motive, public, professed and assumed, and private, unacknowledged and real. This dichotomy interweaves rhetorical narrative from Thucydides onward. So Shakespeare's history plays contrast the high-flown motive of pubic display with backstage chicanery. Such alternation, by nature satirical, aims at motive by attacking the mask of words. The unmasking can occur on a heroic scale, in *Henry V*, or on a small one, in La Rochefoucauld's *Maximes*. Take the argument one step farther and the assumed rhetorical motive becomes more real than the "real" one. Thus Hamlet ponders the contrast between himself and the Player King. The irony has been noted from time to time by the rhetoricians. Quintilian confesses: "Frequenter motus sum, ut me non lacrimae solum deprehenderent, sed pallor et veri similis dolor" (VI, ii, 36). This theme runs through the middle of *Tristram Shandy*. Rhetoric conceived human character to be, like the *topoi*, a series of discrete models, humors, "characters" in the Greek sense. How different this from a romantic uniqueness of the self. The range of selves is limited and, if large, not beyond calculation and catalog. The hobbyhorses can be numbered. Against their typicality, of course, *Tristram Shandy* argues from uniqueness—nothing like any of these people before. The juxtaposition adumbrates the central quarrel between philosophy and rhetoric. It also suggests *Tristram Shandy*'s chronological position, between Augustans and Romantics.

One of the few really good arguments Plato allows the Sophists he gives to Protarchus in the *Philebus* (58b):

> On the many occasions when I used to listen to Gorgias, he regularly said, Socrates, that the art of persuasion was greatly superior to all others, for it subjugated all things not by violence but by willing submission, and was far and away the best of all arts . . .[6]

Plato could never forgive rhetoric for being, as Polus, Thrasymachus, and lesser Platonic villains make clear, built on power. But as Protarchus points out, rhetoric also supplies the principal means of domesticating power struggles, of turning them to peaceful paths. If, as in heroic poetry, rhetorical contest often prefaces a fight, it can substitute for one too. Develop the rhetorical *agon* one step farther and you have logomachy as game, culture as pleasurable.

> It is deeply interesting to see how Isocrates again and again conceives the essence of culture as a purposeless intellectual and spiritual activity—an ideal parallel to that of the gymnastic contests.[7]

The rhetorician's solution to conflict, like the social psychologist's, is talk, verbal confrontation. So it is in *Tristram Shandy*. The violent substratum of the book engages in a constant strug-

[6] Plato, *Philebus*, trans. R. Hackforth, *The Collected Dialogues of Plato*, ed. Edith Hamilton and Huntington Cairns (New York, 1961).
[7] Werner Jaeger, *Paideia: The Ideals of Greek Culture*, trans. Gilbert Highet (Oxford, 1965), III, 78.

gle with rhetoric for control. The implications of rhetoric for a theory of conflict go still deeper. We owe to rhetorical theory the very idea of two-sided conflict. In life, as *Tristram Shandy* makes clear through Toby's counterpointing asides to Walter's schemes and orations, there are usually more than two sides to a dispute. An act of rhetorical will simplifies them to two. It polarizes conflict, makes us play, as Father Ong points out,[8] not to learn but to win. Rhetoric thus provides both theory of conflict and theory of resolution. It also opens out, through debate as game, an immediate access to pleasure, part of the *hēdonē* Gorgias considered the end-product of a mature theory of the *logos*. Following this lead, Sterne was to find his major originality.

The most obvious result of rhetorical training was an intense self-consciousness about language and about man as essentially defined by language. "Perfect rhetoric," Eduard Fraenkel once wrote, "leaves no trace." He could hardly be more wrong. It colors all language, plain or ornate. The debate about rhetorical theory's relation to literature, preoccupied from the beginning with density of verbal decoration, might more profitably have tried to measure the degree of self-consciousness about language, however ornamented. To what degree are we to look at the stylistic surface, to what degree *through* it? If we ponder the surface long enough we become creatures of it. Our reality and our kind of seriousness cease to be philosophic, become rhetorical, limited by language. This is true whether we adore verbal decoration or detest it. If we argue that what is essential to man is his power of speech, then we define a reality finally literary, not philosophic.[9] We find ourselves in the symbolic universe of

[8] Ong, *The Presence of the Word*, pp. 207 ff.

[9] " 'Reality,' for [Gorgias] lies in the human psyche and its malleability and susceptibility to the effects of linguistic corruscation. Thus his rhetoric, though concerned primarily with a technique of verbal elaboration, rests ultimately upon a psychology of literary experience." Charles P. Segal, "Gorgias and the Psychology of the Logos," *Harvard Studies in Classical Philology*, 66 (1962), 110.

Cassirer and Benjamin Lee Whorf. It is an old position of course, one implicit in the traditional argument about the domain of rhetoric and the nature of a true orator. Plato said he knows nothing, Cicero everything. Quintilian asks medially: "cur non tam in eloquentia quam in ratione virtutem eius esse credamus? (II, xx, 9)." The logical domain of rhetoric, given such a definition of man, must be the whole of verbal reality, the verbal, or symbolic component of whatever is to be considered.[10]

Plato's central quarrel with the Sophists came from the conviction that they did not, as Protagoras claimed, make good citizens. A rhetorician might sketch out this reply. (And maintain it, too, as the central justification for Sterne's kind of comedy.) What the rhetorician teaches man is self-consciousness, both of his essential nature as creator and creature of speech, and of his essentially dramatic role-playing self. Such an awareness offers a clear and direct answer to the Socratic injunction to know thyself. It places us in society, teaches the limitations of self, the perpetual posturing that many critics have seen as the essential function of comedy. If it encourages polemic, it channels, controls, deflects it as well. It makes us self-conscious about conflict by formalizing it and, in the process, us too. Comedy finally aims to acculturate us, to harmonize us with society, to make us good citizens. Why not the same argument for rhetoric? Surely this is where the elaborate stylistic play, the rhetoric of *Tristram Shandy*, finally leads. Rhetorical training continued to be given far later than political occasion justified. Historians of rhetoric and of education often wonder why. Perhaps because of its *philosophical* implications. Rhetorical theory was needed be-

---

[10] Quintilian, unhappily, fails to think the problem through at this point. "Ego (neque id sine auctoribus) materiam esse rhetorices iudico omnes res quaecunque ei ad dicendum subiectae erunt. Nam Socrates apud Platonem dicere Gorgiae videtur, non in verbis esse materiam sed in rebus" (II, xxi, 4). Here we surprise Plato in the heart of rhetorical theory itself. The stronger, and proper rhetorical argument contends that words are themselves things, the primary building blocks of our own world.

cause its definition of man was needed as the necessary complement to the philosophical definition. The fundamental Western
dialogue on the nature of man could not otherwise have gone
forward.

> The disagreement between Plato and the sophists over rhetoric
> was not simply an historical contingency, but reflects a funda-
> mental cleavage between two irreconcilable ways of viewing the
> world. There have always been those, especially among philoso-
> phers and religious thinkers, who have emphasized goals and
> absolute standards and have talked much about truth, while
> there have been as many others to whom these concepts seem
> shadowy or imaginary and who find the only certain reality in
> the process of life and the present moment. In general, rhetori-
> cians and orators, with certain distinguished exceptions, have
> held the latter view, which is the logical, if unconscious, basis of
> their common view of art as a response to a rhetorical challenge
> unconstrained by external principles. The difference is not only
> that between Plato and Gorgias, but between Demosthenes and
> Isocrates, Virgil and Ovid, Dante and Petrarch, and perhaps Mil-
> ton and Shakespeare.[11]

Thus the influence of rhetorical theory on imaginative literature
runs deep. It is not largely a matter of stylistic ornament, or of
analysis based on the three styles either. In question is whether
man is the measure of all things, as Protagoras has it, or whether
with Plato (in the *Theatetus*) it is God who performs this function. It is not terribly difficult to see rhetorical narrative when
practiced by classical historians as essential carrier of the relativistic view of man. (No one has done it, however.) It is considerably harder to see it as the central carrier of *the whole
dialogue,* the whole quarrel between philosophy and rhetoric.
Yet it may have been. Certainly we see in *Tristram Shandy* pre-

[11] George Kennedy, *The Art of Persuasion in Greece* (Princeton, 1963),
p. 15.

cisely this quarrel reenacted over its full range. Werner Jaeger, at one point in *Paideia* where he is reviewing the relation of philosophy and rhetoric, stands back a step from the struggle.

> In view of the criticism to which Plato subjects the very principles of sophistic education, we must ask this question: Are religious scepticism and indifference, and moral and metaphysical "relativism," which Plato opposed so bitterly and which made him a fierce and lifelong opponent of the sophists, essential elements of humanism? The question cannot be answered by an individual opinion or preference: it must be objectively answered by history.[12]

Does Sterne not try to answer it with his "history"? Does he not try to sort out the claims of the temporal and the absolute along just these lines? If so, he can be said to climax the older tradition of narrative and to deal in full with that tradition's central concerns and central conflict. "Seriousness" means two different and fundamentally opposed things for philosophical man and rhetorical man. The Victorians wanted *Tristram Shandy* to proselytize for philosophic seriousness. The modern existential critics want *Tristram Shandy* to proselytize for rhetorical seriousness, man's dramatic plight in a relativistic universe. Sterne obliges neither. He rehearses the conflict of the two. Their resolution he finds neither in rhetorical victory nor philosophical wisdom but in the pleasurable reenactment—and pursuit—of both. He finds the midpoint in a state of mind and an activity to which Kenneth Burke has given the brilliant name "pure persuasion." This, Burke says, is something like what the actor feels when he plays for an audience. Something, that is, like what Tristram feels when he plays for us. For that finally is what he is doing. Playing. Into the nature of that puzzling activity we must now make excursus.

[12] Jaeger, *Paideia*, I, 301.

CHAPTER THREE
Games, Play, Seriousness

§

"I will draw my uncle *Toby's* character," Tristram tells us, "from his HOBBY-HORSE" (I, xxiii, 77). And at times he seems to draw everything else from hobbyhorses, too. The metaphor suffuses the book like one of the controlling images Gilbert Norwood finds in Pindar's odes. The play atmosphere it creates has been widely recognized[1] but description of it has not gone beyond the theory of humors. Since there does exist today a body of knowledge called "game theory," it seems reasonable to ask what light it sheds on the game sphere of *Tristram Shandy*. For the kind of seriousness Sterne's *ludus* offers clearly is the seriousness of the gamesman and the game. A satisfactory mapping of the game sphere might grant us common cause with the Victorians, unite the two ways of looking at the novel, the serious and the frivolous. It might explain what high seriousness means in the case of Sterne, and what pleasure means as well. It might even betray how Sterne really offended the Victorians, prompted the immoderate denunciations of Thackeray and Bagehot.

Game theory is not so coherent a body of knowledge as the literary student might wish. It splits into two quite different groups. First we have game theory, properly speaking, invented by the mathematicians and taken over by the social scientists

[1] John M. Stedmond, for example, treats it as a commonplace: *The Comic Art of Laurence Sterne* (Toronto, 1967), p. 100, n. 12.

specializing in conflict-resolution and decision-making.[2] It provides some beguiling metaphors for the literary critic, infinitely expandable yet never so precise as to constrict. But precisely for these reasons, it sometimes only seems to describe, defeats its own purpose. As the mathematicians invented and use it, it provides a consistent body of knowledge. When it is applied to social concerns it becomes tricky, and applied to literature trickier still. Like rhetorical theory, one of its principal contributions to *literary* conflict is in rendering us self-conscious about it. Standing near this internally consistent body of theorizing we

[2] Probability theory deals with games of chance. Mathematical game theory deals with games of strategy. Games of strategy are games where the player must decide what to do rather than let chance decide for him. So we have the definition: "Game theory is a method for the study of decision making in situations of conflict." (Martin Shubik, *Game Theory and Related Approaches to Social Behavior* [New York, 1964], p. 8.) But it works in a carefully defined, very narrow sphere. I have neither space nor competence here to explain game theory even in its simplest outlines. (See, as a beginning, Anatol Rapoport's *Two-Person Game Theory: The Essential Ideas* [Ann Arbor, 1966], and his *Fights, Games, and Debates* [Ann Arbor, 1960].) We must simply state that it tries to provide mathematical models for *rational* conflict. It *assumes* perfectly rational players and, as a cardinal principle, that all players are the same (Rapoport, *Two-Person Game Theory*, p. 126). Every game must have players, payoff, rules. It has six essential features: (1) At least two players; (2) One player begins by moving, this leading to a new situation; (3) New situation determines who moves next and what he can do; (4) Other player's choice is either known or not; if known, the game is one of "perfect information"; (5) There is a termination of the game role; (6) Each player must get a payoff. There are two-person games. There are n-person (more than two-person) games. The second kind is obviously more complex than the first. A zero-sum game is one in which the interests of the two players vary inversely. A non-zero-sum game is one in which interests of the two or more players may at least partially coincide. Mathematical games exist in two forms, an extensive form (written out rules), and a matrix form (charted on a matrix, a mathematical diagram). To be reducible to a matrix and hence to fit into game theory, a game must be very simple. Most of what the layman would call games are far too complicated for treatment by game theory. Special games, in fact, are usually invented for it, the most complicated being the simple kind of dilemma most of us had in our elementary logic class at school. With conflict as it occurs either in ordinary life or in imaginative literature, it cannot deal at all, "because there is no room in that theory for the psychological make up of the participants." (Rapoport, *Two-Person Game Theory*, p. 206).

have a second group which is anything but.[3] One hardly knows what to call it. Anthropologists had cataloged games before *Homo Ludens* but Huizinga's great books seemed to put minds in several disciplines to work in a new way. Jean Piaget had been philosophizing about the role of game but in the relatively narrow arena of child psychology. (See most importantly, *Play, Dreams and Imitation in Childhood.*) Huizinga made the concept as wide as human culture. As a result, we have an important book by Roger Caillois,[4] the more philosophic side of Anatol Rapoport's work (in the volumes cited in n. 2), and recently some literary studies.[5] And, finally, the concept of game has been made into the center of an existential view of the universe.[6]

[3] Perhaps the relation between the two may be clarified by this discussion of the limits of mathematical game theory: "The lesson to be derived [from modern game-theory] is that many of our cherished notions about every problem having an 'answer,' about the existence of a 'best' choice among a set of courses of action, about the power of rational analysis itself, must be relegated to the growing collection of shattered illusions. Rational analysis, for all its inadequacy, is indeed the best instrument of cognition we have. But it often is at its best when it reveals to us the nature of the situation we find ourselves in, even though it may have nothing to tell us about how we ought to behave in this situation. Too much depends on our choice of values, criteria, notions of what is 'rational,' and, last but by no means least, the sort of relationship and communication we establish with the other parties of the 'game.' These choices have nothing to do with the particular game we are playing. They are not *strategic* choices, i.e., choices rationalized in terms of advantages they bestow on us in a particular conflict. Rather they are choices which we make because of the way we view ourselves, and the world, including the other players. The great philosophical value of game theory is in its power to reveal its own incompleteness. Game theoretical analysis, if pursued to its completion, *perforce* leads us to consider other than strategic modes of thought." (*Ibid.*, p. 214.)
[4] Roger Caillois, *Man, Play and Games,* trans. Meyer Barash (Glencoe, Ill., 1961).
[5] See, for example, vol. 41 of *Yale French Studies,* and a challenging book by Michel Beaujour, *Le Jeu de Rabelais* (Editions de l'Herne, n.p., n.d.).
[6] See, for example, two books of oracular—and opaque—wisdom by Kostas Axelos, *Vers la Pensée Planétaire* (Paris, 1964), and *Le Jeu du Monde* (Paris, 1969).

Definitions of play by the nonmathematical theorists are apt to be broad and blurry. *Homo Ludens* offers this one:

> Play is a voluntary activity or occupation executed within certain fixed limits of time and place, according to rules freely accepted but absolutely binding, having its aim in itself and accompanied by a feeling of tension, joy and the consciousness that it is "different" from "ordinary life." Thus defined, the concept seemed capable of embracing everything we call "play" in animals, children and grown-ups: games of strength and skill, inventing games, guessing games, games of chance, exhibitions and performances of all kinds.[7]

But how little this excludes! Anything fits. Even so, how nicely the concept of play fits the unbreachable chasm between Sterne the philosopher and Sterne the jester. The game is utterly frivolous to those without, utterly binding on those within. In itself, it combines the most serious concerns and the least. It manages to be both at the same time.

Caillois gives us a definition of play more immediately germane. Play has six characteristics. It is:

1. free
2. separate
3. uncertain
4. unproductive
5. governed by rules
6. make-believe[8]

The internal conflicts, the seeming inconsistencies, in a definition like this parallel those in *Tristram Shandy*: the combination of

---

[7] J. Huizinga, *Homo Ludens* (Boston, 1955), p. 28.

[8] Caillois, *Man, Play, and Games*, pp. 9–10. A less full definition, offered in a paper by John M. Roberts, Malcolm J. Arth, and Robert R. Bush, "Games and Culture" (*American Anthropologist*, n.s. 61 [1959], 597–605) lists four criteria: (1) competition; (2) two or more sides; (3) criteria for choosing a winner; (4) agreed-on rules.

freedom and governance; unproductivity and high emotional yield; uncertainty and the predictability rules supply; separateness yet the constant need for an audience.

The seeming inconsistencies have not gone unchallenged. R. Ehrmann, in a carefully reasoned reappraisal of Huizinga and Caillois, attacks both for conceiving play in cultural isolation.

> Their formulation of the problem of play makes no allowance for the problem of understanding culture. Culture, *their* idea of culture, is at no time called into question by play. On the contrary, it is *given*: a fixed, stable, pre-existent element, serving as a frame of reference in the evaluation of play. . . . In other words, in an anthropology of play, play cannot be defined by isolating it on the basis of its relationship to an *a priori* reality and culture. To define play is *at the same time* and *in the same movement* to define reality and to define culture.[9]

Ehrmann stresses the social use of play, sees the play-work antithesis as a product of industrialism. The separation of play and culture once denied, it easily follows that "the distinguishing characteristic of reality is that it is played. Play, reality, culture are synonymous and interchangeable.... All of our critical methods must be reconsidered according to these new norms." Under such an extension art becomes simply another kind of play.[10] Such amplification of the game concept destroys its usefulness. Why not call it culture and be done with it? The difference between the two spheres Ehrmann never admits: games are played self-consciously, culture is not. The more self-conscious we are about the restraints of culture, its rules, the more like a game it seems, of course, and the more game can function as absurdist model for culture. But even in advanced existential circles the two stay a long way apart. Culture has, in the long run, its goals

---

[9] R. Ehrmann, "*Homo Ludens* Revisited," in *Yale French Studies*, 41 (1968), 55.

[10] So Beaujour argues in "The Game of Poetics" in the same volume of *Yale French Studies*. "I posit that poetry is a *game*, or like a game," p. 58.

determined for it by time and circumstance. Play exists for its own sake. It may, of course, serve a long-range cultural function, but it does so in virtue of serving an arbitrary short-range one decided on by itself. "The time has come," the editor of the *Yale French Studies* volume noted earlier announces, "to treat play seriously." But if we do so by extending it to equal culture as a whole, we distort its fundamental nature. We may synthesize thereby an agreeable existential view of the world, but we destroy play as a useful descriptive concept.

Precisely the same kind of pressure is being applied to *Tristram Shandy*. Sterne offers a series of games. The Victorians dismiss them as child's play. We insist on taking them seriously; they adumbrate a whole philosophy. The games, first reduced to triviality, are then inflated out of existence. Our problem with *Tristram Shandy*, as with game, is to preserve the middle ground. Huizinga himself, in an essay written several years before *Homo Ludens* appeared, had insisted precisely on this point, both confuting and condemning the wider philosophical view of play:

> The most fundamental characteristic of true play, whether it be a cult, a performance, a contest, or a festivity, is that at a certain moment it is *over*. The spectators go home, the players take off their masks, the performance has ended. And here the evil of our time shows itself. For nowadays play in many cases never ends and hence is not true play. A far-reaching contamination of play and serious activity has taken place. The two spheres are getting mixed. In the activities of an outwardly serious nature hides an element of play. Recognised play, on the other hand, is no longer able to maintain its true play-character as a result of being taken too seriously and being technically over-organised. The indispensable qualities of detachment, artlessness and gladness are thus lost.[11]

[11] Huizinga, *In the Shadow of Tomorrow* (New York, 1964 [1936]), p. 177.

Play, that is, preserves its importance by *not* being serious. To take it as model, as world view, denies its nature. Its peculiar fund of seriousness demands that it not be taken seriously. Perhaps Émile Benveniste has made this point best. "Immense cest le domaine du jeu." Yet this wide scope is not coterminous with all culture: "le jeu est de plus en plus nettement spécifié comme distinct de la réalité, comme non serieux."[12]

Mathematical game theory spans a narrow range very precisely and hypothesizes rational players. The philosophers of play cover a very wide spectrum and hypothesize irrational players, moving from there in great leaps to a universe of the existential absurd. What *Tristram Shandy* requires is a theory between these two, one that allows some of the mathematicians' schematic clarity but does not depend on their—for our purposes crippling—premise of rational players. We have, of course, already discussed just such a one—rhetorical theory.

It is interesting to pair rhetorical theory for a moment with game theory as we have just described it. Both are theories of conflict-analysis and conflict-resolution. Both try to reduce conflict to pattern, defuse it by stylizing it. Both, that is, try to isolate the self-pleasing ingredient in conflict, magnify it, above all make the contending parties aware of it. Both move from persuasion to "pure persuasion." They move from aggression to pleasure, from other to self. They do so by formalizing and distancing conflict. Both move, then, toward a literary definition of reality, toward comedy. Rhetorical *topoi* can, like game "strategies," be categorized. The cocktail-party games that people play, as Eric Berne sees them,[13] are really two- or three-move games from Aristotle's *Topics*. Both are founded on power; both aim to govern the decision-making process. Duncan Black talks of moving from game theory to economic theory to a theory of

[12] Émile Benveniste, "Le Jeu comme structure," *Deucalion*, no. 2 (1947), pp. 161–167.
[13] Eric Berne, *Games People Play* (New York, 1964).

committee decisions, getting at the same time "sufficient means to construct a Theory of Politics."[14] And J. von Neumann and O. Morgenstern, in the classic *Theory of Games and Economic Behavior*: "Our problem is not to determine what ought to happen in pursuance of any set of—necessarily arbitrary—principles, but to investigate where the equilibrium of forces lies."[15] So Isocrates argued against Plato for a political science based on power. Both kinds of theory avoid spontaneous decisions, foresee a strategy for every situation. Rhetorical theory aims to provide strategies for the irrational player against the irrational player, for people as they are. Game theory, restricted to the rational player, can afford much more formal coherence. Both predict the future. (Someone who knows only his own strategy will know the *outcome* but not the *course* of the game. Someone who knows both strategies, however, should be able to predict the course of the game as well.[16] So the theorists at RAND chronicle a future war to avoid it, much as Thucydides chronicled a past one. And their relation to teaching lessons for the future is precisely *Tristram Shandy's* relation to theme. They must remain wholly within the game to teach a lesson to the world outside it. *Tristram Shandy* must abjure thematic statement in order to preserve its theme.) Both equate motive with self-interest.

One is a verbal theory, one nonverbal. To see *Tristram Shandy* in terms of both may work because Sterne both sees words as absolute limit in *Tristram Shandy* and at the same time tries to see beyond them. He tries to see beyond them by ironically juxtaposing the various verbal models of the classical rhetorical tradition: the characters of Toby and Walter; the various genres we have seen; the *topoi*; the styles. Thus from the *disjecta mem-*

[14] Duncan Black, "The Unity of Political and Economic Science," *The Economic Journal*, LX (September 1950), 506–514, reprinted Shubik, *Game Theory*, pp. 110 ff.

[15] J. von Neumann and O. Morgenstern, *Theory of Games and Economic Behavior* (Princeton, 1947), p. 43.

[16] Rapoport, *Two-Person Game Theory*, p. 45.

bra of classical narrative he builds a very modern series of games. By using both kinds of theory—and seeing their fundamental similarities—we can, in a reasonably precise way, surprise Sterne "making it new." We can see, in the narrative tradition in which he chose to write, *Tristram Shandy*'s essential *agon* or game, the struggle of the rhetorical and the philosophical views of man for dominance. We can see Sterne's persistent attempts to move games, the games of philosophy, rhetoric and war, from zero-sum to non-zero-sum (see n. 2). We can see him insisting that philosophical seriousness become rhetorical play.

How does he do so? Rapoport develops a threefold distinction in *Fights, Games and Debates*. "Fight," "game," and "debate" signal for him the three models of conflict. In a fight you try to eliminate your opponent. In a game you reach an accommodation with him—he must be preserved so that the game can continue. Debate offers you a chance to triumph over your opponent's mind, to combine with him, make him of your mind. The end here is not annihilation but absorption. In these terms, Tristram never fights. Dr. Slop must stay on the scene to be pilloried. The tolerancè of *Tristram Shandy*, the geniality of the satire, deprecates fights. The novel comes closest to condemnation, as with the Roman Catholic satire surrounding Slop and his curse, when it represents people who fight rather than play, people, as it seemed to Sterne, of the Roman persuasion. The distinction between game and debate bears more centrally on our purpose. For those who seek—or deny—in *Tristram Shandy* a high seriousness, presume the novel a *debate*, Sterne working us finally toward his persuasion. Practically no one has considered the novel as a *game* in Rapoport's sense of the word, a continuing contest with, by its nature, only intermediate results.[17] We hear a great deal about the novel as process, but that this implies a

[17] As close as anyone has come seems to me Jean Baptiste Suard's review of vols. 7 and 8 (quoted in Alan B. Howes, *Yorick and the Critics: Sterne's Reputation in England, 1760–1866* [New Haven, 1958], p. 18). He calls the novel "a riddle without an object."

new conception of thematic yield seems unconsidered. Yet the satire against learning, the inability of anyone in the novel to convince anyone else of anything, ought to prove something of Sterne's feelings about debates. He seems to have shied away as strongly as he did from fights. His locus lay in game, in the kind of contest offering no final result. The game is over only to begin again. "I shall write," he promises us, "as long as I live."[18] Perhaps this was also what he means when he specified his range as "the laughing part of the world."[19] And when, in his discussion of Sterne, Coleridge tells us that "the laughable is its own end" perhaps he too points to Sterne's contentment with difference, with facing forever an opponent, or a reader, who might not share his mind. *Tristram Shandy*, then, resists the pressures exerted on it from either side of the game sphere. Conflict was not to become physically real (fight), or intellectually so (debate), but to remain in the center.

The best chart for this center I have found is Caillois's four types of games:

1. *agon* (games of competition).
2. *alea* (games of chance).
3. *mimicry* (games of simulation, impersonation).
4. *ilinx* (games involving loss of balance, the sensation of vertigo—drugs, for example, or a ride on a roller coaster).[20]

Surely these are controlling kinds of game in *Tristram Shandy*. Walter contends, Toby simulates a war, Yorick delivers himself to chance, Tristram, as he tells us over and over, makes us and himself giddy. The game of giddines seems especially suggestive for Tristram, perpetually interrupting himself and yet preserving his balance; juggling his sources, yet letting us see them *as*

[18] Laurence Sterne, *Letters of Laurence Sterne*, ed. Lewis P. Curtis (Oxford, 1935), p. 143.
[19] *Ibid.*, p. 189.
[20] Caillois, *Man, Play, and Games*, pp. 14 ff.

sources, so we can appreciate the juggling; disturbing our sense of time by dragging us forward and backward in it; saying one thing to hold our attention while doing another;[21] moving us with a dislocating wrench from one style or one genre to another. ("A ride on a sort of intellectual switchback," Saintsbury calls it.) If we wished to move to biography, we might refer to the *whirl* of London and the *whirl* of Paris, as his social triumphs are described in the *Letters*; or to his continual awareness of the *motions* of his own body, of his blood flowing, his heart beating; or to his unequaled capacity to render the motion of travel, either in the *Letters, Tristram Shandy,* or the *Journey.* Always we feel the attack on our sense of gravity.

The other categories seem hardly less apt. "*Agon,*" Caillois writes, "is a vindication of personal responsibility; *alea* is a negation of the will, a surrender to destiny."[22] Walter's struggles —what do they symbolize but the responsible personality, accountability? And Yorick's collaboration with chance in the incident of the chestnut? The omnipresence of chance makes the whole novel seem a kind of *alea.* Less often discussed than the role of chance in *Tristram Shandy* is the almost pastoral democracy of all those who live under its sway. Time and change do indeed happen to them all, but the conditions of play work precisely against the inequalities of fate. "*Agon* and *alea* imply opposite and somewhat complementary attitudes, but they both obey the same law—the creation for the players of conditions of pure equality denied them in real life."[23] Play both reinforces the force of chance in the novel and supplies a counterforce to it.

It may, then, be possible to view the famous hobbyhorses of *Tristram Shandy* a little more precisely than heretofore, even

[21] "Shandeism is often like a successful conjurer's trick, diverting the attention of the audience from the important part of the transaction." (W. B. C. Watkins, *Perilous Balance* [Princeton, 1939] p. 110.)

[22] Caillois, *Man, Play, and Games,* p. 18.

[23] *Ibid.,* p. 19.

to chart their race. The larger implications already emerge. *Tristram Shandy* has been called a provincial epic.[24] But if it is a collection of overlapping, sometimes conflicting games or hobbies (Walter's, Toby's, Tristram's, Yorick's, Sterne's, Ours) it grows both narrower and more generalized, less localized,[25] becomes the epic of the private life. The game or hobby then becomes the symbol for the private life, and the elements in the novel which challenge and interfere with the games become, inevitably, symbolic of the public life, of duty rather than pleasure. Often comment on the hobbyhorse goes astray just here. Joan Hall remarks that "commitment in the Shandy world is by hobbyhorse."[26] But surely this is the opposite of commitment as we usually use the word. Hobby represents commitment to self, commitment, finally, to pleasure. This point could hardly be more important. If *Tristram Shandy* represents the world *sub specie ludi*, then we can expect to find a world whose pursuit is pleasure. This was, for Sterne, the essential attribute of the private life. Although Tristram asks us continually to reflect on the deal of philosophy beneath his facade of frivolity, when we try, we confront a maze of overlapping games that are nothing but surface, nothing but pleasure. Continually invited to seek the key to the novel, we are continually prevented by the horrid democracy of game. All the games are equal. We can find no *pied à terre*, no fixed point of view. The modern consensus chooses sentiment as the thread out of the maze. But as Norman Holland has pointed out, "Sterne treats sentiment just as he treats every other hobby-horse."[27] Sentiment occurs in the ironic

[24] First by H. Glaesner, "Laurence Sterne," in the *TLS* (1927), pp. 361–362, then two years later by Herbert Read in *The Sense of Glory* (Cambridge, 1929).

[25] Sterne writes to Dodsley, "All locality is taken out of the book" (Sterne, *Letters*, p. 81).

[26] Joan Joffe Hall, "The Hobbyhorsical World of *Tristram Shandy*," *MLQ*, XXIV (1963), 132.

[27] Norman O. Holland, "The Laughter of Laurence Sterne," *Hudson Review*, IX (1956), 430.

context of the whole novel, sentiment indeed, feeling not in excess of the object but for the pleasure of feeling. Feeling, having the right feelings at the right time, becomes as much a game as anything else. Far from connecting man to man, it seems to act the other way, to render man content with the pleasures of his own feelings.

One critic has seen the disparity between theory and practice as central to the novel.[28] The games are in one way all theory and in another all practice. But they are not, precisely not, concerned with the clash between the two. Games stay self-contained, almost autoerotic. They meld theory and practice. The conflict, if there is one in *Tristram Shandy*, must come between the world of individual games and an overall game sense. The crucial question remains whether this point of view exists and, if so, where? In Tristram? Sterne? Us? The search for the central point of view becomes at the last the search for seriousness. To the extent that it can be found, the novel will have a theme (and possibly a structure) in the conventional sense. The theme Tristram announces as his central one, some of the time at least, is motivation. But finding the answer in the game sense, in the private life, casts us out once again onto the opaque surface of the novel, the surface of overlapping games. Motive becomes pleasure and high seriousness is denied us once again. We are thrown back into the lap of comedy.

What kind of morality is possible in such a world? Tristram's genial tolerance seems to be as far as we can go.

> "—*De gustibus non est disputandum*;—that is, there is no disputing against HOBBY-HORSES; and, for my part, I seldom do; nor could I with any sort of grace, had I been an enemy to them at the bottom." [I, viii, 13–14]

Play may sublimate aggression and release sympathy but the

[28] Robert A. Donovan, *The Shaping Vision: Imagination in the English Novel from Defoe to Dickens* (Ithaca, N.Y., 1966), p. 95.

sympathy extends only as far as letting the other fellow play in peace. In this orchestration, the moral sense consists only in becoming aware of the role of hobbies and in the willingness to let each have his own. Some literary implications might be spelled out. Humor becomes preoccupation with a single game and Wit the ability to move with ease and tolerance from one game to another, picking up the rules of one as you let go the rules of the other. But the moral implication goes no further than we have indicated. Once the world has been subdivided into games, there is no center remaining. The logic of *Tristram Shandy* as a fictional form may go further toward solipsism than Sterne, as man or clergyman, would have gone.[29] But the logic stays there. *Really* imbued with the spirit of game (Huizinga says, after all, that the eighteenth century was the great age of play), Sterne differs from us in his stance toward reduction of the world to the private life only. Whereas the modern critic almost instinctively feels the pain of solipsism, of the really private life, Sterne sees its joy, its infinite possibilities for eccentricity. The world of a rigorous individuality his novel creates reduces a modern critic to philosophical despair. Sterne rejoices.

Perhaps we can now see the Victorians' distaste as akin to this modern despair. "Play, love, war, work," writes Kenneth Burke, "these are the names for the ways in which a man is engrossed. The putting of them all together, the 'allocating' of them, is 'religion,' leading to some manner of transcendence or other."[30] *Tristram Shandy* collapses the last three into the first, reduces them all to play, so preventing any transcendence except through it. Perhaps this is what Bagehot really meant when he called Sterne pagan. Allowing no direct access to the other elements of which a transcendence might be composed, he

[29] Perhaps, as Reid says, "his seriousness was greater than he realized himself!" ("The Sad Hilarity of Sterne," *Virginia Quarterly Review*, XXXII [1956], 119).

[30] Kenneth Burke, *Attitudes Toward History* (rev. ed., Boston, 1961), p. 92.

seems to deny seriousness at the source. Arnold observed a parallel configuration in Chaucer's poetry and so denied him a place among the highly serious immortals.[31] And Chaucer and Sterne have in this respect been compared: "Sterne in his human comedy is perhaps closer to the mood and spirit of Chaucer, who is almost always indulgent and tolerant of human frailty.... Chaucer, too, cannot bear remaining overserious for long."[32] The Victorians felt threatened not in their prudishness but in their sense of reality. Inasmuch as they saw him preoccupied by the idea of game, Sterne must have seemed blasphemous. Perhaps this response stands behind the long and widespread disquietude that the author of *Tristram Shandy* was a clergyman. Perhaps, too, the Victorians saw in the exhibitionism of *Tristram Shandy* (and of Sterne) a further disquieting instance of the play impulse. Sterne seemed almost to embody the spirit of display, display for its own sake, as a game. Rolling all this conjecture up into a ball, might we say that the Victorians saw what we have not, that Sterne's novel was an attack on seriousness itself, ours as well as every other kind? More than we do, they may have seen what they most disliked, unashamed addiction to the pleasure principle. If so, they were threatened more fundamentally still. *Tristram Shandy*'s elaborate game with games finally yields a conception of human identity anathema to them. For Sterne, we finally become not only insatiable pleasure-seekers but, by our nature, incurable poseurs. Such a threat to the self, looming behind the condemnation of Sterne's posing, must have seemed gravest of all.

[31] See Richard A. Lanham, "Games, Play, and High Seriousness in Chaucer's Poetry," *English Studies*, vol. XLVIII (1967).
[32] Watkins, *Perilous Balance*, p. 129.

CHAPTER FOUR
The Pleasures of High Seriousness

In the *Encheiridion* of Epictetus, the treatise from which Sterne drew his epigraph for the first volume of *Tristram Shandy*, the philosopher is warned to act out his principles, not prose about them. "Nowhere call yourself philosopher nor speak much among the uninformed about your principles, but act upon them." In Walter Shandy, the commentators seem to agree, Sterne has created an antitype of this ideal portrait, an exhibitionistic, perfectly impotent theorist. "A full account of [his] epic frustrations would," we are told in a recent article[1] "encompass a major part of the novel." He is frustrated as philosopher, as father, as husband, as brother, as orator. Rather than exercising his philosophic principles, he hides behind them, "constantly exacerbated by his inability to control the accidents of everyday existence through his carefully contemplated hypotheses."[2] Plagued, as it seems to him, by chance, his real problems come not from circumstances "but . . . from his own impractical nature."[3] As still another student points out, he is always isolated from the action he wishes to direct.[4] He cannot "bring affairs to

---

[1] A. R. Towers, "Sterne's Cock and Bull Story," *ELH*, XXIV (1957), 25 ff.

[2] John M. Stedmond, *The Comic Art of Laurence Sterne* (Toronto, 1967) p. 82.

[3] Robert A. Donovan, *The Shaping Vision: Imagination in the English Novel from Defoe to Dickens* (Ithaca, N.Y., 1966) p. 104.

[4] William Bowman Piper, *Laurence Sterne* (New York, 1965), p. 59.

a satisfactory conclusion."[5] He can never communicate with his wife, find in her anything but an infinitely yielding, flaccid placidity. This failure is part of a general "failure to communicate, to make the essential connections between himself and the world around him."[6] Like Ovid, he is too witty for his own good: "Walter's hypotheses begin in jest but end in earnest; his judgment at length becomes the dupe of his wit."[7] And, of course, his Ass that Kicks hardly represents the satisfactory sexual orchestration a modern therapist would recommend. Beyond all this, he enacts that most balked and baffled of men, a natural-born orator without an audience. Listen to him Uncle Toby willingly does; appreciate his art he cannot. Finally, if Professor Ralph Rader's rumored speculation is correct, we are to deny Walter even the paternity of Tristram. He becomes the paradigm of modern man, powerless before an indifferent universe but manfully bearing up. Perhaps this side of his character has been sufficiently emphasized. As a corrective, we may want to recall that he does occasionally triumph, does manage, win or lose, to enjoy himself a good deal. He has, after all, chosen to live this way, finds retirement more agreeable than bartering as Turkey merchant with the mysterious Middle East. Walter is impotent, everyone seems to agree, when he confronts the real world. But viewed from the pleasure-principle vantage, this generalization carries less conviction. The novel's point may be this: the world Walter Shandy confronts successfully and with pleasure, the world of speculation, *is* the real world. His successes, not his failures, constitute his *raison d'être*. "Arguments," our author tells us, "however finely spun, can never change the nature of things—very true—so a truce with them."[8] Through Walter, Sterne negotiates his truce in *Tristram Shandy*.

[5] Joan Joffe Hall, "The Hobbyhorsical World of *Tristram Shandy*," *MLQ*, XXIV (1963), 134.
[6] Towers, "Sterne's Cock and Bull Story," p. 26.
[7] John Traugott, *Tristram Shandy's World: Sterne's Philosophic Rhetoric* (Berkeley and Los Angeles, 1954), p. 67.

I

Walter Shandy lacks not only proper audience but proper opponent.[9] Thus he is denied his proper role, the sophist, in both its principal aspects:

> The sophist has two important functions in common with the more ancient type of cultural rector [the *vates*]: his business is to exhibit his amazing knowledge, the mysteries of his craft, and at the same time to defeat his rival in public contest. Thus the two main factors of social play in archaic society are present in him: glorious exhibitionism and agonistic aspiration.[10]

He cannot properly combat; he cannot properly display. No wonder he tries to head off chance,[11] to tilt against fate. What other opponent does he have? His predicament put in this way backlights the essential issue—the pleasure he gains from his learned struggles. The most obvious instance of this pleasure, and the most widely discussed, offers itself in the description of Shandy Hall receiving the news of Brother Bobby's death. (*Tristram Shandy*, V, ii, 348 ff.) Tristram does his best to prohibit us from real sorrow. Bobby is never alive enough to die, and his death enters and leaves apropos nothing. All the light shines on Walter's coping with *his* sorrow. Tristram aims to tell us, that is, less how all occasions do inform against his father than how his father deals with this particular occasion. Tristram gives us the paradigm for Walter's strategy in an anecdote interpolated within the interpolation:

> My father had a favourite little mare, which he had consigned over to a most beautiful Arabian horse, in order to have a pad

---

[8] Laurence Sterne, *Letters of Laurence Sterne*, ed. Lewis C. Curtis (Oxford, 1935), p. 18.

[9] "Walter spent most of his time in the rhetorical field. There were a thousand notions to defend against no one." (Traugott, *Tristram Shandy's World*, p. 60.)

[10] J. Huizinga, *Homo Ludens* (Boston, 1955), p. 146.

[11] Piper, *Laurence Sterne*, p. 50.

out of her for his own riding: he was sanguine in all his projects; so talked about his pad every day with as absolute a security, as if it had been reared, broke,—and bridled and saddled at his door ready for mounting. By some neglect or other in *Obadiah*, it so fell out, that my father's expectations were answered with nothing better than a mule, and as ugly a beast of the kind as ever was produced.

My mother and my uncle *Toby* expected my father would be the death of *Obadiah*—and that there never would be an end of the disaster.—See here! you rascal, cried my father, pointing to the mule, what you have done!—It was not me, said *Obadiah*. —How do I know that? replied my father.

Triumph swam in my father's eyes, at the repartee—the *Attic* salt brought water into them—and so *Obadiah* heard no more about it.

Now let us go back to my brother's death. [V, iii, 352–353]

Walter's pleasure in his own joke shields Obadiah from retribution. It also restores Walter's good temper, converts his exasperation into pleasure. A like conversion occurs in the oration on Bobby's death. Instead of weeping, "My father managed his affliction otherwise" (V, iii, 351). He talks it away. And often, Tristram makes clear, eloquence creates pleasure in excess of the painful occasion:

Provided an occasion in life would but permit him to shew his talents, or say either a wise thing, a witty, or a shrewd one— (bating the case of a systematick misfortune)—he had all he wanted.—A blessing which tied up my father's tongue, and a misfortune which set it loose with a good grace, were pretty equal: sometimes, indeed, the misfortune was the better of the two; for instance, where the pleasure of the harangue was as *ten*, and the pain of the misfortune but as *five*—my father gained half in half, and consequently was as well again off, as it never had befallen him. [V, iii, 352]

Now it is true that, as a philosopher, Walter does not cope very well with a chancy experience. He does not explain or illuminate either death or Bobby's death. Yet in a way—and this is Tristram's point—he is doing very well, making himself comfortable with an event he cannot alter. Philosophy and eloquence together do not cope with or change experience but they make him easy in the face of it. For, as Tristram says: "Philosophy has a fine saying for every thing.—For *Death* it has an entire set" (V, iii, 353). Tristram alludes, before setting his father leafing through these, to a well-known instance of grief in antiquity: Cicero's grief for his daughter Tullia. To assuage it, he had compiled his famous, now lost, *Consolatio*. It may be, as H. J. Rose sardonically notes, that even while overcome by grief Cicero remained sufficiently proud of his eloquence to point out to Atticus that only he, Cicero, had ever thought of writing a *consolatio* to himself.[12] Still, he was profoundly grieved and did seriously harrow the philosophical wisdom to find some consolation for Tullia's death. He found none that directly relieved his sorrow, of course, but did find, as many a man had found before him, that the work itself somewhat eased his heart. Tristram travesties this:

> But as soon as he began to look into the stores of philosophy, and consider how many excellent things might be said upon the occasion—no body upon earth can conceive, says the great orator, how happy, how joyful it made me. [V, iii, 351–352]

The travesty serves to introduce his father's *consolatio*, which *is* an easy one. For Walter Shandy thinks of the consolations of philosophy not as nuggets of wisdom but as nuggets of rhetoric, proverbs each one more satisfying to the mouth than the last. The wisdom does not console. The words do. Even the order of the discourse does not really matter:

> the misery was, they all at once rushed into my father's head,

[12] H. J. Rose, *A Handbook of Latin Literature*, 3d ed. (London, 1961), p. 189.

that 'twas difficult to string them together, so as to make any thing of a consistent show out of them.—He took them as they came. [V, iii, 353]

Walter then runs through his tricks, Toby contributing his usual idiot's chorus. But we should not think Walter defeated by Toby's incomprehension, frustrated. He becomes his own audience and succeeds magnificently. By the end "he had absolutely forgot my brother *Bobby*" (V, iii, 356). He succeeds where Cicero had failed.

Readers who find Walter a paradigm of frustration may be bringing to the novel a conception of rhetoric—or more largely of language—different from that which Tristram brings. We tend to think that language communicates conceptual truth. Such manages the world. Not much managing gets done in *Tristram Shandy*, and one naturally concludes that language is at fault, that, as Traugott brilliantly makes clear, the book is in fact *about* how language is at fault. But if we think of language as, essentially, not controlling concept but yielding pleasure— and Tristram conceives of it in this way—much of the frustration evaporates. The occasion here is death and Walter has a grand time with it. What more could any philosopher do? If language continually fools us—and Tristram is often at pains to tell us that it does—here we are getting back some of our own. Perhaps it is still fooling us, but at least it is in a pleasurable way.

We can call Sterne's humor philosophical in this sense if we will. It clearly is meant as something for us to generalize upon. Yet I hardly think he saw this kind of thing as what man should or should not do, so much as simply what he does do. He is not at all cheering us up in the way Thackeray thought—or some modern critics think—the humorous moralist should do. He is simply telling us how language is used, how—let us vary the wisdom of a modern popular philosopher—what is spoken is often less important than the act of speaking. The operative force is not philosophy but rhetoric, not wisdom but pleasure. Perhaps this will be clearer if we look at how the news is received in the kitchen.

Tristram contrasts the two orators for us, lest we miss it.

> A curious observer of nature, had he been worth the inventory of all *Job's* stock—though by the bye, *your curious observers are seldom worth a groat*—would have given the half of it, to have heard Corporal *Trim* and my father, two orators so contrasted by nature and education, haranguing over the same bier.
>
> My father a man of deep reading—prompt memory—with *Cato*, and *Seneca*, and *Epictetus* at his fingers ends.—
>
> The corporal—with nothing—to remember—of no deeper reading than his muster-roll—or greater names at his finger's end, than the contents of it.
>
> The one proceeding from period to period, by metaphor and allusion, and striking the fancy as he went along, (as men of wit and fancy do) with the entertainment and pleasantry of his pictures and images.
>
> The other, without wit or antithesis, or point, or turn, this way or that; but leaving the images on one side, and the pictures on the other, going strait forwards as nature could lead him, to the heart. O *Trim!* would to heaven thou had'st a better historian!—would!—thy historian had a better pair of breeches!—O ye criticks! will nothing melt you? [V, vi, 359]

We are to be melted. What avails a sermon to the head compared with five words to the heart: "Are we not here now, continued the corporal ... —and are we not—(dropping his hat upon the ground) gone! in a moment!—" (V, vii, 361). In case any of us has slipped the punch of this sequence, Trim works it again and Tristram tells us that the world hangs upon it.

> Now as I perceive plainly, that the preservation of our constitution in church and state,—and possibly the preservation of the whole world—or what is the same thing, the distribution and balance of its property and power, may in time to come depend greatly upon the right understanding of this stroke of the cor-

poral's eloquence—I do demand your attention,—your worships and reverences, for any ten pages together, take them where you will in any other part of the work, shall sleep for it at your ease. [V, vii, 361]

A mild joke is to be harvested in Trim's using the same kinds of rhetorical devices Walter Shandy uses, changing only the direction of their allusion downward. Nature generates the same tricks Cicero does and with the same result.[13] Eloquence overcomes and discharges the sorrow. Walter is his own audience; Trim has an external one. Walter's joy comes from the sound of his own voice, Trim's from the pathos that his infinitely moving ethos elicits from his fellow servants. Both, however, cope with the sorrow in the same way, both unpack their heart with words. Before anyone in the kitchen is free to take a sentimental bath in Trim's eloquence, Tristram shows them all swiftly interpreting the news in terms of their own interest and pleasure. If we were on the search for sincerity in *Tristram Shandy*, surely we could do no better than the scullion's reply to the news: "He is dead! said *Obadiah*,—he is certainly dead!—So am not I, said the foolish scullion." Once the essential self has resettled in terms of the news, the tears and speeches can start. We are not angels, Tristram tells us, but "men cloathed with bodies, and governed by our imaginations." We are at liberty, I suppose, to find the center of this twin oratorical occasion in Trim's sentiment rather than Walter's display, to meditate, as Tristram beseeches us, upon Trim's hat. Yet the novel has quite as much to do with display as with sentiment and the two seems to be carefully balanced here. (Tristram says earlier of Trim: "The fellow lov'd to advise,—or rather to hear himself talk" (II, v, 95). All the fuss at the end of chapter VII about the eloquence versus the dripping of sentiment seems a false issue. What one sees in either

[13] William J. Farrell, "Nature Versus Art as a Comic Pattern in *Tristram Shandy*," *ELH*, XXX (1963), 29.

case is a speech that converts the disturbance and fear death creates into a pleasurable eloquence, a pleasurable sorrow. The consensus of present-day students of Sterne is that sentiment saves a bleak world, connects man and man where words cannot.[14] Where Walter Shandy's eloquence fails, Trim's succeeds. As a general one for all Sterne's work, this proposition falls outside our scope. As a particular one applied to this scene, it seems demonstrably wrong. What saves man in the face of death is the impenetrable coat of his own egotism, his ready willingness to put sorrow into the service of pleasure. Neither Tristram nor Sterne carries the matter farther than this. We are offered an eloquent trap and a sentimental trap. If we escape both, we are free to do as the characters do, to be amused and moved by death. To watch it controlled by humor. To enjoy it.

Wasserman invested the episode with broader, chillier import:

> But the news that Brother Bobby was dead had as many discrete meanings as the hobby-horses the auditors rode, And each rode a different one.
>
> In Tristram's world, meaning had become a function of each person's private, subjective concerns, which alone remained as an interpretive organization. . . . What is more, in this completely individualistic world none of the private principles ever succeeds in organizing life, and chaos is forever breaking in.[15]

Doesn't Sterne look farther than this? The news indeed splits into individual response. And individual response must be served. The ego protects itself. We see this being done. But Sterne does not, as Wasserman does, and as commentators generally tend to, stop here. He shows us the self-indulgence liberating real feeling. The end of the scene is grief, social com-

---

[14] See, as best example, Traugott's introduction to *Laurence Sterne: A Collection of Critical Essays* (Englewood Cliffs, N.J., 1968).

[15] Earl R. Wasserman, *The Subtler Language* (Baltimore, 1959), p. 170.

munion. The communication can come because the ego has been served, grief rendered self-serving, pleasurable:

—Nature is nature, said *Jonathan*.—And that is the reason, cried *Susannah*, I so much pity my mistress.—She will never get the better of it.—Now I pity the captain the most of any one in the family, answered *Trim*.—Madam will get ease of heart in weeping,—and the Squire in talking about it,—but my poor master will keep it all in silence to himself.—I shall hear him sigh in his bed for a whole month together, as he did for lieutenant *Le Fever*. [V, x, 365]

They take off, this kitchen of chaos, into a common warm bath of real sympathy that leads, naturally, to the delicious sorrow of retelling Le Fever's death. Sterne points to how people receive death, absorb it, become whole again, a *community* once more. Do not expect people to be selfless *at first* under a blow. See how they *make themselves so*, how the ego contrives it. Seeing a chaos of individuality here plainly means expecting more of people than Sterne did. As Trim says (if indeed it is he who speaks here):

—Now I love you for this—and 'tis this delicious mixture within you which makes you dear creatures what you are—and he who hates you for it—all I can say of the matter, is—That he has either a pumkin for his head—or a pippin for his heart,—and whenever he is dissected 'twill be found so. [V, ix, 364)

In *this* mixture lies the real humor of the scene, not in the more mechanical hat trick, the rhetorical gesture, the comparison of finite and infinite, great and little that critics, following Coleridge, have found central to Sterne's humor.[16] Sterne has often

[16] For example: "What, of course, gives the scene that incongruity in which humor lies, is the use of Trim's gesture with his hat as a symbol of mortality: that is, the equating of the trivial with the serious, the unimportant with the important." (Dorothy Van Ghent, *The English Novel: Form and Function* [New York, 1961], p. 94.) Surely the quarry is bigger than this.

been accused of having taken refuge in illusions ("especially in the imaginative dramatization which is Shandeism")[17] when life became unbearable. The scene just explored offers the precisely opposite circumstance. Accommodation, acceptance, not illusion, stand center stage. Cohesion results, not chaos, not individuality but community. Critics have simply not followed the novel all the way. They have stopped where, as good existential moderns, they have been taught (by forces *outside the novel*) to stop. Alan D. McKillop says, for example:

> In spite of overriding obsessions, human ends are infinitely various, but we may say that in *Shandy* the ends are sexual satisfaction, the riding of hobbyhorses, and the full expression of ideas and sentiments.[18]

Deferring judgment on the first of these, the last two we have now seen, at least once, not as ends but as means. The characters in the novel do not see them that way. Be clear about that. We do.

We surprise Walter Shandy at his game of making himself easy even more plainly in the excommunicating curse (III, x, 167 ff.). It all starts with Slop's failing to play the game of Obadiah's knots. Chance tied them, of course, Obadiah being here as elsewhere a humble servant. And they become, needless to say, knots of destiny:

> In the case of these *knots* then, and of the several obstructions, which, may it please your reverences, such knots cast in our way in getting through life—every hasty man can whip out his penknife and cut through them.—'Tis wrong. Believe me, Sirs, the most virtuous way, and which both reason and conscience

[17] W. B. C. Watkins, *Perilous Balance* (Princeton, 1939), p. 109. See also, for example, Norman N. Holland, "The Laughter of Laurence Sterne," *Hudson Review*, IX (1956), 430.

[18] Alan D. McKillop, *The Early Masters of English Fiction* (Lawrence, Kan., 1956), p. 206.

dictate—is to take our teeth or our fingers to them.—Dr. *Slop* had lost his teeth . . . he tried his fingers—alas! the nails of his fingers and thumbs were cut close . . . Lend me your penknife—I must e'en cut the knots at last - - - - - pugh! - - - psha! - - - Lord! I have cut my thumb quite across to the very bone—curse the fellow—if there was not another man midwife within fifty miles—I am undone for this bout—I wish the scoundrel hang'd—I wish he was shot—I wish all the devils in hell had him for a blockhead—

The allegory depicts Slop as lacking game sense. Tristram, at least, takes pains to generalize the knots within the passage and, via a pun just before the passage, to alert us to "the second *implication*[19] of them . . . I hope you apprehend me." If Sterne makes art out of his anti-Catholic prejudices in the novel —and I am not clear that he does—surely it is by making the Church, through its humble servant Slop, the spoilsport in the novel, the absolutism that would deny each man his hobbyhorse in peace and quiet. The game sense seems here to represent elasticity of human judgment, the sense of proportion that Slop's absolutism denies him. For this deficiency, he must be saddled with the curse. Walter's response reveals "a great respect for *Obadiah*," the immediate object of the cannonade, but also "some little respect for himself." "Had Dr. *Slop* cut any part about him, but his thumb—my father had pass'd it by—his prudence had triumphed: as it was, he was determined to have his revenge." Tristram's meaning, if I am not falling into one of his traps, must be that Slop, by disabling himself for midwifery, has intensified his offense. As expiation, he gets a lecture on cursing for ease and pleasure. "I seldom swear or curse at all—I hold it bad," Walter tells him, "but if I fall into it, by surprize, I generally retain so much presence of mind . . . as to make it answer my purpose—that is, I swear on, till I find myself easy." The move-

[19] Sterne's Latin puns, as here with *implico*, have not been so fully discussed as they might be.

ment from Slop's practice to Walter's theory rehearses the central movement of the novel—from fighting to game, from aggressive, outward gesture to conversion into pleasure within. Once you are easy, as Walter makes clear, proportion follows. You can make a *proper* connection with the outside stimulus. To improve the joke—and the lesson—Walter then makes Slop read the curse aloud. The literary context of the reading exemplifies *Tristram Shandy*'s method of converting high seriousness downward into pleasure. The document itself could hardly be more serious, the style more resonant. Surely this is why Tristram gives us the rumbling Latin periods even though Slop actually reads the English translation.

> Ex auctoritate Dei omnipotentis, Patris et Filij, et Spiritus Sancti, et sanctorum canonum, sanctaeque et intemeratae Virginis Dei genetricis Mariae,
>
> —Atque omnium coelestium virtutum, angelorum, archangelorum, thronorum, dominationum, potestatuum. . . .

It is, par excellence, a document from the public world, and we witness its full domestication into that private life that constitutes the specialty of Shandy Hall. First Toby supplies melodic accompaniment by whistling Lillabullero—the *Argumentum Fistulatorium* (the windy argument, we might translate), the characteristic retreat, in the novel, to the paradise within—throughout its recitation.[20] The curse's dignity is further undermined by its being offered in two languages at once. Inevitably we compare them. We are thus forced to attend to linguistic surface first, to meaning only secondarily. Further, the recitation's mechanistic inflexibility, its final *inapplicability* to the private life, is emphasized by the mechanical insertion of (*Obadiah*) where needed, and by the supplying of the proper pronominal equivalents throughout in the same kind of parentheses.

---

[20] "You must know it was the usual channel thro' which his passions got vent, when anything shocked or surprised him—But especially when anything, which he deem'd very absurd, was offered."

The device works even more effectively in the Latin text by being printed above the line. There are other interruptions. Toby breaks in with "for my own part, I could not have a heart to curse my dog so." And with musical accompaniment comes the neutral, deflating terminology of the practicing amateur musician: "[Here my uncle *Toby* taking the advantage of a *minim* in the second barr of his tune, kept whistling one continual note to the end of the sentence—Dr. *Slop* with his division of curses moving under him, like a running bass all the way.]" The terrible maledictions become a consort of viols, a peaceful home entertainment in the great age of amateurism. Pastime the Shandy brothers, plus Tristram, manage to make of it; they attack its aggression, turn it from fight into game, savor the rhetoric.

We might profitably fix Sterne's aim in an episode like this less in high seriousness directly than in the high style, with all its resonances of the solemn, important, public world. As well as tying the curse to diminished object and diminished occasion, and playing games with its extreme periodicity, Sterne has a little fun with, for example, that favorite classical game of ornament through terminations, *homoioptoton* and *homoioteleuton*:

Maledictus sit vivendo, moriendo ————————————

————	————	————	————	————
————	————	————	————	————
————	————	————	————	————
————	————	————	————	————

manducando, bibendo, esuriendo, sitiendo, jejunando, dormitando, dormiendo, vigilando, ambulando, stando, sedendo, jacendo, operando, quiescendo, mingendo, cacando, flebotomando.

The figures supposed to add dignity and melody inject here only pomposity. They do not work directly on the audience, but ironically. Toby responds with feeling, but not the feelings the style aims to create. For him, it backfires. And Walter relishes it in another way—he becomes an ironical connoisseur. Both, then, turn the rhetoric to their own purposes, draw its fangs. Together, they constitute a small society making war against spoilsport solemnity of language, rendering its aggression harmless through comic irony.

Characteristically, Tristram does not leave even Walter's prose unscrutinized. He continues in the following chapter (xii):

> Now don't let us give ourselves a parcel of airs, and pretend that the oaths we make free with in this land of liberty of ours are our own; and because we have the spirit to swear them,—imagine that we have had the wit to invent them too.
>
> I'll undertake this moment to prove it to any man in the world, except to a connoisseur;—though I declare I object only to a connoisseur in swearing.

Then he is off to finish his transition and give a swipe to the critics. But in passing he gives us a swipe too. For we have, like Walter, become connoisseurs in swearing. We laugh at Slop's, and the curses's, formularity. Yet we all (curses being traditional, infinitely repeatable) are as conventional as Slop's rendition, though on a less amusing scale. We too are stupid, mechanical, inelastic. We are not even—lest we give ourselves airs—very good connoisseurs either. The language of the passage—it can, I think, bear our analysis and then some—mocks us for priding ourselves both on our spontaneity and our considered contemplation. Tristram has, that is, first a Bergsonian laugh at inelasticity then, like Kierkegaard, chuckles at our naïve admiration of spontaneity and denigration of the pleasures of repetition—which we, after all, have been sampling throughout the passage. It thus illustrates two opposite theories of comedy at once. We are invited to feel superior, become connoisseurs, then rebuked for being so. We finally become the comic dupes ourselves, inevitably mistaken. Such is Tristram's game, to have it both ways, to mock us coming and going.

Walter Shandy's other projects and imaginative burdens lend themselves to the same kind of interpretation we have applied to his *consolatio*. Thus in the *Tristrapaedia*, for whose writing he neglects Tristram's more necessary and domestic *paideia*, we can look at him as essentially pleasing himself. He goes through torments in the writing, of course, but remains within himself, pursues an activity whose reward remains within himself. He fathers, in it and through it, an ideal child, becomes too an ideal father. "I was my father's last stake," Tristram tells us, ". . . and accordingly my father gave himself up to it with as much devotion as ever my uncle *Toby* had done to his doctrine of projectils.—The difference between them was, that my uncle *Toby* drew his whole knowledge of projectils from *Nicholas Tartaglia*—My father spun his, every thread of it, out of his own brain" (V, xvi, 372).

Walter's misapprehension of the world provides Sterne with a running mild satire on mankind, but more important is the way the misapprehension works. It works to integrate and re-affirm the personality. Here is one of Tristram's comments on his father's relation to ideas:

> It is a singular blessing, that nature has form'd the mind of man with the same happy backwardness and renitency against con-viction, which is observed in old dogs,—"of not learning new tricks."
>
> What a shuttlecock of a fellow would the greatest philosopher that ever existed, be whisk'd into at once, did he read such books, and observe such facts, and think such thoughts, as would eter-nally be making him change sides!
>
> Now, my father, as I told you last year, detested all this.—He pick'd up an opinion, Sir, as a man in a state of nature picks up an apple.—It becomes his own,—and if he is a man of spirit, he would lose his life rather than give it up. [III, xxxiv, 221]

Ideas to Walter are not essentially true or false but pleasurable. The ordinary philosopher who gathers his apples according to the reality principle copes more satisfactorily with reality, but Walter, we may claim, copes far better with himself. Since it is *dogmata* rather than *pragmata*, thoughts rather than deeds, which trouble men, he addresses himself to the *dogmata*. Something like this point is made by Walter Houghton's excellent article on "The English Virtuoso in the Seventeenth Century."[21] By a virtuoso, Houghton tells us, things are studied for the marvels they yield, for the pleasure they give the student rather than for the systematic truth they are made to yield up. Stedmond, who discusses this article, classes Walter Shandy as "a burlesque of the decadent virtuoso." A burlesque he is, and the comic exaggeration that creates the burlesque lies precisely in the gusto and enjoyment with which Walter Shandy makes ideas his own. But surely this is common. Scholars are always entertaining theories because the theories entertain them. There is nothing decadent about it. It is natural to man. And that it has so markedly not been bred out of Walter Shandy is, I suspect, one of the reasons we grow fond of him. We feel with him when he does enjoy himself as well as when he fails to.

Walter Shandy, typed as we have him in terms of the pleasure principle, cuts a cockeyed figure as philosopher. As philosopher, as someone trying to know the world, he is clearly as hapless as the critics would have him. ("Never man crucified TRUTH, at the rate he did" [IX, xxxiii, 644].) If we consider him under the first character Tristram gives him, however, his type seems a good deal more poised: "he was born an orator;—Θεοδίδακτος" (I, xix, 51–52). And the first duty of the Orator born is not to find out the truth or control the world but to *win the argument*. Here, by Tristram's report and our own observation, he was not so hapless:

> Persuasion hung upon his lips, and the elements of Logick and Rhetorick were so blended up in him,—and, withall, he had so

---

[21] Walter E. Houghton, Jr., "The English Virtuoso in the Seventeenth Century," *JHI*, III (1942).

shrewd a guess at the weaknesses and passions of his respondent, —that NATURE might have stood up and said,—"This man is eloquent."

The ironic qualification supplied by the Shakespearean echo begins Tristram's, and the novel's, treatment of the theme of eloquence. The virtuous life, as Antony describes it of Brutus, is replaced by a natural talent for disputation.[22] His father, Tristram takes pains to tell us, has had no training. ("My father was never at a loss what to say to any man, upon any subject" [V, xxxiv, 395].) Like his brother Toby in another way, he is a natural. This leads him to become a particular kind of orator— the champion of odd notions. The genesis of this habit, as Tristram conjectures it, is of particular importance for the conception of Walter's character we are trying to develop:

—for he had a thousand little sceptical notions of the comick kind to defend,—most of which notions, I verily believe, at first enter'd upon the footing of mere whims, and of a *vive la Bagatelle*; and as such he would make merry with them for half an hour or so, and having sharpen'd his wit upon 'em, dismiss them till another day.

I mention this, not only as matter of hypothesis or conjecture upon the progress and establishment of my father's many odd opinions,—but as a warning to the learned reader against the indiscreet reception of such guests, who, after a free and undisturbed enterance, for some years, into our brains,—at length claim a kind of settlement there,—working sometimes like yeast;— but more generally after the manner of the gentle passion, beginning in jest,—but ending in downright earnest.

Whether this was the case of the singularity of my father's notions,—or that his judgment, at length, became the dupe of his

[22] "His life was gentle, and the elements / So mixed in him that Nature might stand up / And say to all the world, "This was a man!' " (*Julius Caesar*, V, v.)

wit;—or how far, in many of his notions, he might, tho' odd, be absolutely right;—the reader, as he comes at them, shall decide. All that I maintain here, is, that in this one, of the influence of Christian names, however it gain'd footing, he was serious;—he was all uniformity;—he was systematical, and, like all systematick reasoners, he would move both heaven and earth, and twist and torture every thing in nature to support his hypothesis. In a word, I repeat it over again;—he was serious. [I, xix, 53]

So runs the anatomy of Walter's seriousness. It was, Tristram tells us, like falling in love. Clearly he is all right until he becomes serious. Then his judgment falls victim to his wit. While in the game sphere he is safe. It is hard to resist drawing a parallel here with Toby, safe in his garden, in one kind of love; then getting serious—and into trouble—about another.

For both men, the proper domain is gratification, the game of pleasure. Can we deny to Walter, considered from this point of view, as much pleasure in his game as Toby takes from his? To see the world perpetually through a favorite hypothesis is to convert everything therein to your own pleasure:

> It is the nature of an hypothesis, when once a man has conceived it, that it assimilates every thing to itself as proper nourishment; and, from the first moment of your begetting it, it generally grows the stronger by every thing you see, hear, read, or understand. This is of great use. [II, xix, 151]

The sexual metaphor here as in the previous passage is no accident. Walter's successful lovelife is with words, and next to it his fabled sexual misadventures count very little.

II

If Walter Shandy, then, "proposed infinite pleasure to himself" in "reasoning upon every thing which happened" (III, xviii, 189),[23] it was in the zealous pursuit, not of truth, but of elo-

---

[23] Walter is forever being described as "hugely tickled" or "hugely pleased" at his new projects.

quence, that he proposed to find it. Nothing, indeed, in *Tristram Shandy* more deserves remark than Tristram's attitude toward the hypothesis. It figures not as thing of truth but as thing of use. It is an object. Tristram feels a good deal more self-conscious than Walter about this duplicity, of course. Still, even Walter can regret (about noses, III, xli, 239) "that truth can only be on one side." The stress of the novel falls, then, less on what Walter says than on how he says it. His hypotheses, which have bemused us all, seem less important in this view than the framework of their presentation. It may be that, by attacking the whole range of Walter Shandy's crackpot theories, Sterne calls into question theorizing per se, attacking, we might say, high seriousness itself. But if so, he does it as with the curse by attacking the *mechanism* of high seriousness directly, by mounting an attack on the high style. Surely toward this all the parody of formal rhetorical devices tends. Farrell has made clear[24] how conscious Tristram wants us to be about Walter's use of them. We are to be, as he says, connoisseurs like Spenser's E. K. Sterne wants, finally, comically to discount the high style, the tradition of eloquence as a vehicle for high seriousness, by pointing out its role as end rather than means. He points to its pleasure-giving rather than its truth-telling function.[25] Tristram mourns, in the third volume (xiv, 185), the decay of eloquence. It is tempting to argue from this remark to a comic version of the novel's statement about eloquence, to see it as no longer useful for the public world, no longer effective communication. It

[24] Farrell, "Nature Versus Art," p. 18.
[25] Here I am, if I understand him correctly, in flat disagreement with Traugott. He points to the same self-consciousness about ornament, but sees it performing a much more serious function. "This is Sterne's curious conduct of rhetoric; whereas it is ordinarily a discursive rather than an intuitive art (as De Quincy points out), by Sterne's bringing rhetorical effects into consciousness by naming them, rhetoric becomes an intuitive, almost poetic, art, since the discursive quality becomes *not* an end in itself but a *symbol* of human communication" (*Tristram Shandy's World*, p. 112).

remains only as meaningless game. Such an interpretation, agreeable as it is to our thesis here, fails again to follow Sterne to the end. The novel betrays less *regret* at the failure of eloquence to serve the public world than *joy* at its potential for the private one. The irreducible minimum for language to which Sterne points is once again pleasure. This, at all events, cannot be taken from us, whatever the truth may be. As Huizinga puts it, in terms of play:

> Play cannot be denied. You can deny, if you like, nearly all abstractions: justice, beauty, truth, goodness, mind, God. You can deny seriousness, but not play.[26]

We should resist any attempt to place *Tristram Shandy* at the tag end of a historical development of the high style, to say that by Sterne's time, formal eloquence was fit matter only for joking. He seems to be saying, instead, that we are still taking it *too seriously*. It is tempting to see in Sterne a pleader for the plain style. There is scattered evidence for it:[27] "The highest stretch of improvement a single word is capable of," Walter Shandy tells us, "is a high metaphor,—for which, in my opinion, the idea is generally the worse, and not the better" (V, xlii, 405). And Tristram contributes a little rant:

> I hate set dissertations,—and above all things in the world, 'tis one of the silliest things in one of them, to darken your hypothesis by placing a number of tall, opake words, one before another, in a right line, betwixt your own and your reader's conception,— when in all likelihood, if you had looked about, you might have seen something standing, or hanging up, which would have cleared the point at once. [III, xx, 200]

But this philosophy of style is hardly taught by the novel as a

---

[26] Huizinga, *Homo Ludens*, p. 3.
[27] He occasionally pleads for it in the *Letters*. But sometimes, as in the highly contrived context of the "Journal to Eliza" (Sterne, *Letters*, p. 316), we wonder how serious he can be.

whole. It provides a lesson in precisely the kind of opaque style Tristram condemns. It does not apotheosize ornament, to be sure, but rather stylistic self-consciousness. The conventional division of style into high, middle, and low has lasted, miraculously for such an imprecise classification, well into our own time. The principles of categorization upon which it was based have seldom been clear and have varied, in any case, from theorist to theorist. But density of figurative ornament, complexity of syntax, and dignity of subject have usually been at the center. *Tristram Shandy*, in its stylistic implications, sweeps this whole framework of categories away, substituting in its place one based on stylistic self-consciousness. At one end we have the straight reader, deaf to irony, who takes every appeal and every gesture at its face value. In *Tristram Shandy*, Toby obviously creates this role, the walking literal.[28] On a neutral spectrum of style, it would be represented by the purely denotative style, transparent, which one ignores in haste for the facts beneath. Truman Capote's *In Cold Blood* has, I suppose, re-created this style for our time. At the other end of the scale in *Tristram Shandy* stands Tristram himself. Nothing fools him. He takes nothing at face value. He personifies, in this drama, the master stylistic debunker. On our scale of stylistic theory, the prose of Joyce might form this extreme. And, in such a redefinition of style, two such strangers as Hemingway and Faulkner would meet—for in the degree that each asks us to consider his style as style, to look at its surface and not beneath it, they are much alike. In the middle of *Tristram Shandy*'s range we must place Walter Shandy. Far from blind to manner and means, he still lets matter stand in the forefront of his imagination.

Such a spectrum of self-consciousness about style has no high

[28] We would add here the critics who have read *Tristram Shandy* in this way as well as those, for example, who read the rhetorical gesture *au grand serieux*, as "the psycho-physical crossroads of life," or who think of gesture as the novel's eloquence beyond words.

or low in the older sense. There seems, that is, no reason to applaud a self-conscious style more than one choosing to operate in the opposite mode. But does not *Tristram Shandy*, by implication at least, really set up such a range of invidious discriminations? Logically it ought not to be so. As to self-consciousness about style, if it does not free us from convention, ought it not at least offer us a free choice among conventions? But the impetus of Sterne's novel moves in the opposite direction. Stylistic self-consciousness is a virtue and comes to stand for perception into motive. Inasmuch as Tristram can discount the rhetoric of both Walter and Toby, he is their superior. And, by strong implication, the same relation should hold true between Tristram and us. For surely rhetorical custom comes to have a larger resonance as the novel goes on, comes to stand for the customs of language as a whole. It is not just any vocabulary of behavior to play games with, but *the* vocabulary. And the awareness of rhetoric's rules seems almost a paradigm for comic awareness itself, the awareness of society's rules, their artifice and necessity. For Sterne is no Romantic. The path to spontaneity runs through artifice, not around it. Sterne saw society and individual identity as both essentially dramatic in origin and function. The theory of oratory and the practice of oratorical narrative come as close as the novel gets to offering the rules for the dramatic presentation.

Walter Shandy then, natural-born orator and good natural (and moral) philosopher (II, vii, 101), combines in his person the quarrel between philosophy and rhetoric. And through him Sterne resolves the argument. Both are pursued for pleasure. Persuasion and truth both turn inward. Both serve the self. Walter is not only a "great MOTIVE-MONGER" (458) but a great exemplar of motive as well. Through him Sterne syncretizes the dispute endemic to the literary kind he chose to work in. Real eloquence in *Tristram Shandy* is enjoyable eloquence.

Real philosophy comes to mean tolerance of the game sphere.[29] Although when grief touches his lips, Walter is scarcely distinguishable from Socrates (V, xiii, 370), at other times the two diverge somewhat. The injustice done to Isocrates is as great. The name of the game is no more persuasion than it is truth.

We might end these reflections on Walter as comic pattern of eloquence, *vir bonus imperitus dicendi,* with a statement by Kenneth Burke on the self-conscious prose style of one of Sterne's predecessors in ironical fiction:

> I sometimes wonder, for instance, whether the "artificial" speech of John Lyly might perhaps be "truer" than the revelations of Dostoevsky. Certainly at its best, in its feeling for a statement which returns upon itself, which attempts the systole to a diastole, it *could* be much truer than Dostoevsky. And if it is not, it fails not through a mistake of Lyly's aesthetic, but because Lyly was a man poor in character, whereas Dostoevsky was rich and complex.[30]

Both points bear strongly upon *Tristram Shandy,* the turning in upon itself and the pressure that it puts on (*pace* the Victorians) the depth and richness Sterne's character so magnificently supplies. If we deny high seriousness in the way that Walter Shandy's character and utterance, as Tristram presents them, do deny it, then we must sooner or later ask what is left to *talk about.* And we then recoil to the pure center of literature—to words themselves. Following Traugott's discussion, Donovan[31] and Sigurd Burckhardt[32] have discussed words as things, language as subject, in *Tristram Shandy.* But if we are going to cast

[29] Surely this is the meaning of the puzzling passage at the end of chap. viii in Volume V.

[30] Kenneth Burke, *Counter-Statement,* 2d. ed. (Chicago, 1957), pp. 42–43.

[31] Donovan, *The Shaping Vision,* pp. 95–96.

[32] Sigurd Burckhardt, "Tristram Shandy's Law of Gravity," *ELH,* vol. XXVIII (1961).

Sterne as the last great defender of the classical word, we must add why he defended it. Not to communicate but to enjoy. In *Tristram Shandy*, people speak, yes, and gesture too, to enjoy themselves. It may be that from such enjoyment communication follows, that pleasure liberates real fellow-feeling. But when Sterne teaches this lesson, through Toby, he also makes clear that pleasure must come first, pleasure that prepares for and triggers the comic alternative to man's predicament. This holds true for all the major characters. They may represent each a side of Sterne himself. And thematic pattern certainly connects them.[33] Yet what connects them still more firmly is their resolute search for (and success in finding—the book is after all a comedy) pleasure. For Walter, it lay in *agon*, contest and victory. For Toby, it lay in mimesis, in a pastoral impersonation of war.

[33] "He gives us—in Toby, Walter, and Yorick—curiously reduced versions of the great aspirations of soldier, scholar, and priest." (Martin Price, *To the Palace of Wisdom* [New York, 1964], p. 320.)

CHAPTER FIVE
Pastoral War

Uncle Toby is the great triumph of *Tristram Shandy*, the figure all have applauded, that none could resist loving. In the thin times for Sterne's reputation, when the stock of learned wit was low or self-conscious clowning thought exhibitionistic, Toby carried the novel and the novelist on his sturdy shoulders to the next period of critical appreciation. To the Victorians, he proved that Sterne could feel deeply, that the core of the man was not beyond redemption. And to the modern commentator, he stands for that sentiment that glues together—barely but nobly—the fragmented bits of an existentially absurd world. As humor character, as gamesman par excellence in the novel, he is—exaggerated as his obsession may be—essentially like us all:

> Yet this impossible artifact, Toby, becomes by Sterne's dramatic rhetoric a strangely real and sane man, whose desperate humors we see finally as essentially no different from Walter's, or, indeed, from those of Madam or His Worship the Reader.[1]

Sterne is not urging us to be like Toby,[2] yet we must come to see that in many ways we are like him. He is obsessed by game as we are—only more so. Obversely, he is full of fellow-feeling as we should be—only more so. Hence his humor and his pa-

---

[1] John M. Traugott, *Tristram Shandy's World: Sterne's Philosophic Rhetoric* (Berkeley and Los Angeles, 1954), p. 33.
[2] *Ibid.*, p. 74.

thetic glory. Toby is, then, crucial to those who find the novel serious and equally so to those who think Sterne a jester, a miniature painter in the pathetic vein. For so important a character in either argument, he has been more often pointed to, smiled with, applauded, loved, than analyzed. Toby is crucial to our argument, too. And since we proceeded, in the case of Walter Shandy, on Kenneth Burke's principle of "perspective by incongruity" and considered him not as philosopher so much as gamesman, here it seems more promising to consider Toby not as gamesman but as philosopher. For this role he is, after all, a natural.

I

Toby begins his fabled hobbyhorse, as a philosopher should, to answer a two-headed question. Where was he wounded? He finds out. And he cures himself in the finding. Thus he starts his cure not by an act of feeling, but by an act of knowing. He does research. He becomes, in fact, the only successful, authentic virtuoso in the novel. He makes of his knowledge first a healing nostrum, then a game, a perfect paradigm for the satisfactions of private life. A. R. Towers points out that the fortifications are given a pronounced sexual character, are Toby's "woman" long before the Widow Wadman comes along.[3] And, arguing more generally, Burckhardt maintains that "manifestly the chief structural metaphor of the novel [is] the interchangeability of sex and war."[4]

Thus his game satisfies precisely the drive his wound prevents him from satisfying. And in his satisfaction, he stumbles on—by experience—what Walter Shandy tries to search out in theory— the wellspring of human motive. Walter may be the ideal con-

[3] A. R. Towers, "Sterne's Cock and Bull Story," *ELH*, XXIV (1957), pp. 20 ff.
[4] Sigurd Burckhardt, "*Tristram Shandy's* Law of Gravity," *ELH*, XXVIII, I (1961), p. 82.

templative man.[5] But it is Toby who finds the secret of the private life. Although remarkable for the depth of his feeling, not of his thinking, he challenges the reader to think about as well as love him. For his real significance lies, not in how deeply, sincerely he feels—a quality that we can only admire, wonder at—but in how he finds happiness, in his game of pastoral war and *its* relation to his spontaneous fellow-feeling. Although Toby may not be a systematic philosopher, he is a successful one and it is as this that we are first invited to consider him.

One is continually tempted, on the basis of one part or another of *Tristram Shandy*, to make Sterne out a prophet. The temptation is especially strong with Toby, the model for today's private man. Pleasure in private life has more and more been drawn from a carefully controlled virtuosity, from one kind of hobby or another. The pleasure is passive and indirect, the aim contentment. Toby is thus the perfect complement to his brother, who draws his contentment from struggle. Yet the brothers are fundamentally obsessed not by the search for wisdom but by the play attitude. This has not been the common view. Stedmond, for example, contrasts the two brothers this way:

> But Toby is represented as interested in knowledge for its own sake, as a sort of therapy, rather than in any practical application of it. He plays at war in order to undo the damage which war has done to him. . . .
>
> Walter is something else again. His fence against life is the realm of pure abstraction. In this realm, theory is ostensibly designed to lend order to the flux of existence. In fact, of course, his theories are of as little practical use as Toby's model forts, perhaps even less, since Toby does find ease and contentment in his miniature bowling green world. . . . Neither succeeds in living up to man's full potentiality, and their idiosyncrasies are accordingly comic. Both can succeed only by anaesthetizing parts of

[5] Robert A. Donovan, *The Shaping Vision: Imagination in the English Novel from Defoe to Dickens* (Ithaca, N.Y., 1966), p. 105.

themselves, by refusing in their varying ways to accept the full consequence of the human state.[6]

But Walter, too, plays therapeutic games. Both brothers live a pastoral life in a green world. Neither acknowledges the existence of a "reality" outside the range of his possible pleasures. Both are, in our sense of the word as well as Sterne's, "retired." Both, like Shandy Hall itself, reflect the game sphere's absence of economic pressure and of the resulting extrinsic profit. For both, the struggles are over. More so, I think, than any other eighteenth-century novel, *Tristram Shandy* is the novel of private life. Public events are few. Walter Shandy rises and falls from arcane reading, Toby from a gazette, yet both lead, from a public perspective, a private, derived, secondary existence. We may, I suppose, talk about their not accepting "the full consequences of the human state." But those consequences, whatever they are, are nowhere suggested in *Tristram Shandy*. Its sphere *is* the game sphere. This is its reality. Neither brother evades it. And, if Walter's perpetual frustration includes a pleasurable alloy, Toby's placid contentment does not lack its stresses.

He does, after all, feel called upon to defend his hobby, to apologize for making a hobby out of war. The dumb man speaks. This itself is surprising, and we wonder at the end of it whether "Lillabulero" isn't his *forte* after all. Walter had been twitting him about that loss of his hobbyhorse which the peace of Utrecht had occasioned. "My uncle *Toby*," Tristram tells us, "never took this back-stroke of my father's at his hobby horse kindly.—He thought the stroke ungenerous; and the more so, because in striking the horse, he hit the rider too, and in the most dishonorable part a blow could fall" (VI, xxxi, 458). The most dishonorable part is presumably Toby's martial honor, but I suppose we must make it a physical part too, and so symboli-

[6] John M. Stedmond, *The Comic Art of Laurence Sterne* (Toronto, 1967), pp. 81–83.

cal of the hobby as a compensation for the wound and the sexual impotency that the wound brings (if it does) with it. Walter means presumably that Toby is willing to continue a cruel and bloody war so that he may continue his own hobby. Toby takes the criticism far otherwise. He defends real war, his real career as a soldier. A thirst for glory does not equal, he insists, a thirst for blood. "Or because, brother *Shandy*, my blood flew out into the camp, and my heart panted for war,—was it a proof it could not ache for the distresses of war too? O brother! 'tis one thing for a soldier to gather laurels,—and 'tis another to scatter cypress." Toby then defends war as an instrument of national policy:

> Need I be told, dear *Yorick*, as I was by you, in *Le Fever's* funeral sermon, *That so soft and gentle a creature, born to love, to mercy, and kindness, as man is, was not shaped for this?—* But why did you not add, *Yorick*,—if not by NATURE—that he is so by NECESSITY?—For what is war? what is it, *Yorick*, when fought as ours has been, upon principles of *liberty*, and upon principles of *honour*—what is it, but the getting together of quiet and harmless people, with their swords in their hands, to keep the ambitious and the turbulent within bounds? And heaven is my witness, brother *Shandy*, that the pleasure I have taken in these things,—and that infinite delight, in particular, which has attended my sieges in my bowling green, has arose within me, and I hope in the corporal too, from the consciousness we both had, that in carrying them on, we were answering the great ends of our creation. [VI, xxxii, 462]

It is not always easy, in *Tristram Shandy*, to separate Sterne from Tristram, and I do not think Sterne kept or wanted to keep a constant distance between them. Here they seem some way apart. Toby is deluded. His delight in war is uncritical, naïve, illogical. The English are a quiet and harmless people driven by necessity to curb turbulent ambition. Yet the principal motivation that spurs on these quiet and harmless people, Toby among them, is turbulent ambition and thirst for glory. Toby is defending the *necessity* of war, yet the occasion of his defense is a regret that peace has been made, that war is no longer a necessity. The Utrecht treaty that Toby thought base, made precisely the point Toby addressed himself to—that war was not necessary, was being continued for the reasons of honor that, Toby confesses, are really what gratify him. One can, I think, safely conclude that Toby disproves—and we are intended to see (though Tristram does not see) that he disproves—his own argument. Yet Toby, after all, is hardly a Tamburlaine. What actually charms him at the beginning is the *play* aspect of war—the drums, guns, and ensigns. These he reckons harmless, easily agreeing with his dependable compassion. He is right. But he leaves the aggression out of war, the pleasures taken from it outside the play sphere. He turns a fight into a game. Here is his naïveté, a naïveté his brother cannot understand. Toby remains consistent within his own terms and Tristram accepts these, presumably, and applauds them. At least he never really brings the two opinions together, whereas Sterne, I think—or the novel if you will—insists that we do.

No one, so far as I know, has ever asked why Sterne chose to give a character like Toby a martial hobbyhorse.[7] This incongruity Toby addresses himself to in his apologetical oration: sentimental sympathy versus killing. At the end of the oration, it still confronts us. Toby has been for so long a sentimental darling, one step away from the village idiot perhaps, but loved the more for it, that only temerity might suggest him as allegorizing an unpleasant truth. He is, rather, the redeeming feature of the universe. Watkins, for example, writes of Sterne's conviction, "not unlike that of Coleridge and especially of Wordsworth, that the principal spirit in the Universe is one of joy.... The perfect

[7] A life-model argument has been suggested. See the letter of Reginald L. Hine, F.S.A., to *TLS* (21 May 1931), p. 408 for the suggestion of Captain Robert Hinde as an original.

embodiment of this spirit, the perfect child of nature is, of course, Uncle Toby."[8] A child of nature he is, but of a less Romantic nature than this. He reenacts, as homely truth, the powerlessness of sentiment, of humane fellow-feeling, at the hands of the natural, centrally-human propensity for game. Toby is in a very real sense an idiot, *idiōtēs*, obsessed by the private life. On his hobbyhorse, he has no fellow-feelings at all. Stedmond, in a fine discussion of this side of Toby's nature, maintains that "Tristram, in fact, makes a distinction between Toby's *moral* character and his *hobby-horsical* character."[9] Does he not rather shirk the problem and make us put the two together ourselves? We are to conclude, I suspect, that the pleasures of the one are essentially egotistical, that one plays a game for one's own satisfaction, fights a war for the pleasure it gives one. The long diapason of sentiment for Toby has been accompanied by a good deal of praise for him as a humorous character. The mechanical dependability of his responses, his one-track mind, certainly earn him this. But the drastic constriction, the absorption in his game really liberates his feelings, gives them a marvelous freedom and openness. Sterne was, I think, fearful of man's natural propensity to make game of experience because of its power to cut off the flow of feeling at the wellspring. Once one fell into a role, the natural feelings were replaced, the old poseur knew, by others quite different. At the same time, he saw the enormous moral value of Toby's pastoral warfare in draining off the aggressive and aesthetic drives that tend to capitalize on the feelings and put them to nefarious use. For the paradox of Toby's war is a double one. It is both a *peaceful* and an *artistic* war, that constitutes, as Traugott says,[10] Toby's rhetoric, and a very full one too. Only by means of it can

---

[8] W. B. C. Watkins, *A Perilous Balance* (Princeton, 1939), pp. 118–119.
[9] Stedmond, *Comic Art*, p. 60.
[10] Traugott, *Tristram Shandy's World*, p. 18.

Toby feel with the purity and absence of calculation which has made him so loved and eulogized.

A reassembled Toby, the two sides of his character put together, figures forth a character different from that of the popular imagination and more complex. Toby is made to play war because war, better than any other game, illustrates the power of game itself. He would not be the same character if obsessed by say, ordinary gardening, or if he "followed the turf" in the usual meaning of the phrase, although he perhaps might be as dear to those readers whose ideas of sentimental humor take a Dickensian turn. Game and sentiment conflict in his character as much as war and sentiment. Toby's sentiment, his fellow-feeling, can be as pure and spontaneous as it is because his game —even though it is a game played out, on the real stage, in hideous suffering—so fully satisfies him. The fortifications may be his mistress. If so, he made a lucky choice. She satisfies him completely. And it is the complete satisfaction that liberates his feelings. Toby's feelings appeal because uncontaminated by egotism. Not naturally pure of heart, "a comic version of the saint,"[11] as popular opinion has it, he has become so when his egotism has been drained off. The whole of Toby's character is a purity of feeling bought *at the price of* obsession. Sterne is far, I think, from sentimental gush about Toby. He is emphatically not a lovely person who also is by chance a half-wit with a shell-shocked hobby.[12] He can be the one only because he is the other. And this appears to Sterne a generic verdict. It will always be thus. Perhaps, for Sterne, sentiment redeemed a radically unknowable world. But, looking at Toby, we may doubt it. The price is too high.

We might ask a derivative question. What kind of comment

[11] Stedmond, *Comic Art*, p. 81.
[12] Even so ardent an admirer as J. B. Priestley has written: "He is the simplest of mortals, and, indeed, one step further along the path of simplicity and he would be tumbling into idiocy." (*The English Comic Characters* [New York, 1925], p. 145.)

about war, rather than about Toby, does his apologetical oration, and the hobby behind it, really make? The answer is not far to seek. All that is good about war survives transplanting to the bowling green and the sooner the better. For the bowling green war is not less absorbent of aggression than real war but more so. Sterne sees, I think, Toby's war as a kind of applied pastorality, using the mechanism of pastoral to discharge quite unpastoral impulses. Such a pastoral is less a resignation than a working-through of antisocial behavior. Perhaps in this connection we can see the juxtaposition of the two brothers a little more clearly. It is not really a question of either one's realizing his full potential as a human being. Neither stands as the round character of realistic fiction. Sterne uses them in a narrower drama. A drama of sentiment. Toby has managed to liberate his sentiment, can feel spontaneously for others. Walter can feel for others only occasionally and upon specific stimulus. This difference has up to now been accepted as simply a difference in temperament, a *donnée*. Actually, the novel earns it. Toby has managed to invest his game with all the demands of his ego, and it has satisfied them. Walter's games are less completely relied upon and so less successful. They are, at the same time, more pretentious and intellectual. Here is mild satire, if you like. Philosophy, supposed to lead to love, contentment, tranquillity, leads to puzzlement instead. War, supposed to lead to hatred, instead takes us to the goals of philosophy. But such an observation can hardly be optimistic in the usual sense. The root of the ethic of fellow-feeling in *Tristram Shandy* is indeed a spontaneous goodness in the heart of man. But that is not all that is at the heart of man. Self and desire share the place and must be satisfied. What satisfies them is pleasure. Even in war, the ultimate antisocial behavior, we find a salve to the self, a satisfaction, which liberates fellow-feeling. Soldiers are, and can be, so sentimental, Sterne tells us, because the other side of their job so fully and satisfactorily orchestrates that part of the psyche that interferes with spontaneous fellow-feeling. As General Lee said, it is good war is so horrible, else we would grow too fond of it.

Perhaps this argument may clarify a final question that remains about Uncle Toby: the relation of his sentiment to his humor, or rather of our sentimental response to him and our humorous response. Dilworth, in his illuminating and entertaining (and not very intelligently reviewed) *The Unsentimental Journey of Laurence Sterne*, discriminates between these two absolutely.[13] In the matter of the fly, for example, he is at pains to point (correctly, I think) to the artifice and affectation of the rhetorical structure surrounding the famous liberation scene. The whole, he thinks, is made up as a self-conscious exercise. And, "let it be said flatly . . . and with all possible resolution, that the episode of Uncle Toby and the Fly is not sentimentality but humor."[14] I do not see how the two can be separated, coming as they do from a single source. A distinguished scholar has shown us that the affected side of humor and the eccentric side can yield quite different results: "That humour as imitation and affectation should be ridiculous, while humour as particular inclination, individual uniqueness, or even individual eccentricity should be held above ridicule, will surprise nobody who has read widely in the age of Pope."[15] We can see how Sterne elicits the second and not the first. We trust the spontaneity of Toby's response, whereas in anyone else we would call it affected, because we accept from the beginning not simply the sentimental side of him but the *Kriegspiel* side, and put them together. Toby's "humor" is really two things, his bowling green

---

[13] Maack's Hegelian resolution of the two gives up and calls it "literary magic"! (Rudolph Maack, *Laurence Sterne im Lichte seine Zeit* [Hamburg, 1936].)

[14] Ernest N. Dilworth, *The Unsentimental Journey of Laurence Sterne* (New York, 1948), p. 27.

[15] Edward N. Hooker, "Humour in the Age of Pope," *HLQ*, XI (1948), 372.

and his spontaneous goodness. His goodness, his sentimentality, if you will, is as much a part of his humor as his dependable interest in siege works. The success of Toby as a character of the popular imagination surely comes from just this union of a goodness and a frivolity equally dependable and from the same cause. Inevitably, we attribute an equal causality to each side of his nature. Now, we can accept eccentric preoccupation far more easily than we can believe in spontaneous goodness. By yoking them—and providing a *reason* why they should be yoked —Sterne can transfer our acceptance from the one to the other. Suddenly a spontaneous goodness does seem to come from the heart of things. And, because this is as it ought to be, the eccentricity, too, seems to be as it ought to be. Toby as a humor character, then, seems to me explicable, not simply a happy accident, or a random marriage of quirk and sentimental goodness. Perhaps the theoretical relation of the two will be clear if we quote a theorist, Hazlitt on humor: "The most curious problem of all, is this truth of absurdity to itself. That reason and good sense should be consistent is not wonderful: but that caprice and whim, and fantastical prejudice, should be uniform and infallible in their results, is the surprising thing." People, he goes on, make an aesthetic response to the wholeness and consistency of humor. "The devotion to nonsense, and enthusiasm about trifles, is highly affecting as a moral lesson: it is one of the striking weaknesses and greatest happinesses of our nature. That which excites so lively and lasting an interest in itself, even though it should not be wisdom, is not despicable in the sight of reason and humanity." Sterne, it seems to me, is trying to say, in the case of Toby, just why the absurdity is true to itself. He succeeded: Hazlitt, just after this passage, alludes to Uncle Toby as the kind of character he has in mind.

We face, then, a problem. Hazlitt, if I understand him, thinks humor a far more natural product than wit: "Humour is, as it were, the growth of nature and accident; wit is the product of art and fancy. Humour, as it is shown in books, is an imitation of the natural or acquired absurdities of mankind . . . wit is the illustrating and heightening the sense of that absurdity by some sudden and unexpected likeness or opposition of one thing to another."[16] By this definition, at least, as well as by the analysis we have pursued above, Toby finally challenges not our humor but our wit. Witty he is not. But the relation of his two humors seems to me to be—and to be intended to be—a profoundly witty one.

II

"There are two play-idealizations par excellence," Huizinga tells us, "two 'Golden Ages of Play' as we might call them: the pastoral life and the chivalrous life."[17] Toby, by bringing the arts of war (more properly of the siege, the most ritualized scenario war then provided) into his garden, unites them. And from their union springs the spontaneous sentiment that has made him famous. He is not a great figure of humor because he can feel, but he can feel because he is a great figure of humor. If Walter Shandy shows that the truth of human affairs hides from the purely speculative reason, then Toby shows it hidden from pure feeling too. Once again we are thrown back on the metaphor of drama for society and identity. It alone combines reason and feeling. McKillop reminds us that Sterne was the first novelist to write a *humorous* novel that would be called sentimental.[18] How the humorous and the sentimental find their common ground and their causal connection in pleasure is, I hope, by now clear. We may, then, apply it to some of the critical discussions Toby's characterization has generated. It prompts

[16] *Lectures on the Comic Writers:* I–"On Wit and Humour," *The Collected Works of William Hazlitt,* ed. A. R. Waller and Arnold Glover (London, 1903), VIII, 11, 15.

[17] J. Huizinga, *Homo Ludens* (Boston, 1955), pp. 180–181.

[18] Alan D. McKillop, *The Early Masters of English Fiction* (Lawrence, Kan., 1956), p. 182.

first an observation on the kind of humor Sterne creates. The best definition of humor I know is Kenneth Burke's:

> Humor is the opposite of the heroic. The heroic promotes acceptance by *magnification*, making the hero's character as great as the situation he confronts, and fortifying the non-heroic individual vicariously, by identification with the hero; but humor reverses the process: it takes up the slack between the momentousness of the situation and the feebleness of those in the situation by *dwarfing the situation*. It converts downwards, as the heroic converts upwards. Hence it does not make for so completely well-rounded a frame of acceptance as comedy, since it tends to gauge the situation falsely. In this respect it is close to sentimentality, a kinship that may explain why so many of our outstanding comedians (who are really humorists) have a fondness for antithetical lapses into orgies of the tearful.[19]

A conventional definition like this illuminates the unconventional kind of humor Toby represents. There is little conversion downward; the situation is most artificially dwarfed but scaled at the start to fit Toby. And, he copes very well with what he has gathered from coincidence. Not the *discrepancy* but the *fittingness* between man and situation seems Sterne's target. Toby preserves the Bergsonian mechanized response of the humor character, its inelasticity, but the private life seems made to contain it. He gauges circumstance well, not ill. Thus the final stress falls not on Toby but on Shandy Hall, on the private life. *It* is humorous. The discrepancy finally springs from the relation of public and private worlds and this relation enters only by implication into *Tristram Shandy*.

Toby's hobbyhorse backlights the whole civilizing tendency of game, its ability to metamorphose aggression, to move in on the arena of fight. Stedmond precisely misses the point when he says of Toby's garden war: "The tendency to treat human

[19] Kenneth Burke, *Attitudes Toward History* (rev. ed., Boston, 1961), p. 43.

beings as 'things,' evident in Uncle Toby's dehumanized version of war, is a dominant strand in the book."[20] Humanize, not dehumanize, is surely the right word. Toby's pity finds a precise analogy in his pastoral siege, his movement of warfare from the public sphere to the private.

Toby may also shed ironic wisdom on that great and for him soporific philosopher John Locke. Tristram is holding forth in a Lockian way (II, iii, 85 ff.) when he tells us that Toby's life "was put in jeopardy by words." The double sense of *where* he was wounded is in question. The general reflection is on the dangers of ambiguity inherent in the nature of words. But Toby's experience teaches the opposite lesson—the chance healing words can effect. What they take away, they with equal frequency give. We compare Locke's despair at the absurd world with Toby's mindless, unerring march toward pleasure. Toby may be the mental eunuch he seems, but so what? Not what he knows but what he shows predominates. Here evaporates another perplexity associated with Toby. We are often told of his inarticulateness. He cannot speak. He must gesture. Most of the novel's readers must at one time or another have asked themselves liverishly what he might say could he speak. Expressing nothing, nothing to express. If Sterne's people cannot really understand one another, they do not have much to communicate either. But neither what they have to say nor how they say it is as important in *Tristram Shandy* as how each of the characters pleases himself. Communication, if not irrelevant, hardly preoccupies us.

We might consider what Toby's presence adds to the novel's great scenes of sentiment. There are three levels to those, a critic tells us: the dominant conscious-pathetic; the alternative farcical; the recessive tragic.[21] Clearly Toby supplies the first and

[20] Stedmond, *Comic Art*, p. 60.
[21] Ben Reid, "The Sad Hilarity of Sterne," *Virginia Quarterly Review*, XXXII (1956), 117–118.

Tristram the second. To admit the recessive tragic would drag us back into high seriousness. But we do blend Toby's perspective with Tristram's into a point of view neither can supply alone. Consider, for example, the sentimental pathos in the scene of scenes, the death of Le Fever (VI, vi, 416 ff.). We need not rehearse again the ways Tristram qualifies the scene with obvious irony. The unstated irony clusters round Toby's head. For all of Le Fever's tribulations come from following the greater shadow of Toby's hobby, from going to the wars. Yet Toby's pity can be qualified precisely for this reason. He accepts the logic of game (Le Fever *must* go to the wars) and the obligation to pity him, with equal openness. He can thus muster a heart-whole pity that the ironical Tristram cannot. It remains for the reader to contrast the two attitudes, to locate the springs of Toby's kind of fellow-feeling and the springs of Tristram's. The debate about whether Sterne wants us to read the pathos straight (as the Victorians did) or ironically (as today), thus seems a false distinction. The passage suggests rather the possibility of *both kinds* of response, the source and nature of each.[22] The scene offers two handles. We grasp whichever suits us. If, grasping neither, we observe both, we can syncretize the Victorian reading of Sterne's sentiment with the modern. Of course he shows us feeling enjoyed for its own sake. And of course he shows Tristram laughing at such enjoyment. Of course he does not laugh at Toby but at us. We must imitate both attitudes—the feeling and the laughter—to hold them together in our minds. Through such artifice lies *the reader*'s path to redemption, to spontaneous response. We must fall into neither rhetorical trap, the sentimental nor the ironical. We must see instead, or at least first, the groundwork of sentiment and of irony. If we are simply ironical, we are on the modern road to high seriousness. If simply sentimental, we will shortly fall in love with Toby, and this is

[22] What these are for Tristram we shall consider in the next chapter.

fatal. We must keep the two views separate. Stedmond points to similarity:

> There is an obvious analogy between this "world" created by Toby, and Tristram Shandy's "world" of words. Tristram, too, fends off the spleen by transforming his trials and tribulations into symbolic form.[23]

But the gross resemblance hides a multitude of differences. They play different, almost antithetical games, and the differences stand out much more boldly than the likenesses. For Tristram is a clerk and the clerical game has always stood aloof from the chivalric. To this game of words, to the narrative structure of *Tristram Shandy*, we must now turn.

[23] Stedmond, *Comic Art*, p. 120.

CHAPTER SIX
The Self-Serving Narrator

ა
ჳ

I

Tristram's fondness for philosophically justified digression has bemused his admirers into overlooking the older narrative pattern from which the digressions depart. For all his joking about Locke's history-book, Tristram was writing one himself, an intellectual autobiography. His proceedings will be those of a classic chronicler, he declares early in Book I:

> He will have views and prospects to himself perpetually solliciting his eye, which he can no more help standing still to look at than he can fly; he will moreover have various
>
> > Accounts to reconcile:
> > Anecdotes to pick up:
> > Inscriptions to make out:
> > Stories to weave in:
> > Traditions to sift:
> > Personages to call upon:
> > Panegyricks to paste up at this door . . .
>
> To sum up all; there are archives at every stage to be look'd into, and rolls, records, documents, and endless genealogies, which justice ever and anon calls him back to stay the reading of:—In short, there is no end of it;—for my own part, I declare I have been at it these six weeks, making all the speed I possibly could,—and am not yet born:—I have just been able, and that's all, to tell you *when* it happen'd, but not *how*;—so that you see the thing is yet far from being accomplished. [I, xv, 37]

However jocular this declaration of purpose, and however much he later departed from it, it shows Tristram looking back to the kind of Herodotean narrative discussed earlier. The classical historians had shown him a very different kind of pattern, one where narrative gave way at regular intervals to rhetorical occasion. Whether fictionalized public debate, oracle, formal character, apostrophic moral reflection, or narrative digression in the high style, these interruptions all offered opportunity for indirect, ironical commentary on the chronicle they interrupted. Such an interruption—Thucydides' Pericles praising the Athenians, Livy's Hannibal rallying his troops, or Sallust's Cato exhibiting his antique yet sterile virtue—hardly digresses in the usual sense of the word. It stands as part of the narrative rather than ornament to it. Tristram puts this narrative lesson to two uses. He borrows the integral digression for himself; he borrows the narrative-digression-narrative-digression pattern for his Father and Uncle Toby. The chronicles of both proceed by narrative descriptions, comment plus generalization, alternating with the highly dramatic set pieces that make *Tristram Shandy* so easily excerptable. Tristram, introducing Toby, will tell us of his great modesty, then later show it in action, show it transmuting, for example, Le Fever's embarrassing manner of death into a tableau incapable of making a young person blush. Or he will let his father develop one of his "thousand little sceptical notions of the comick kind," in an apostrophe, then contrast notion and subsequent behavior. The reader, much as with Thucydides, Livy, or Sallust, must keep on his toes, continually compare telling and showing. The comparison often aims for irony. As with the historians (and with Shakespeare the historian) we become self-conscious about the rhetorical occasion, develop a feeling for the backstage. In this narrative tradition, context is crucial and excerpting the primal curse. So with *Tristram Shandy*. The sentimental bouquet-gatherer, like Gielgud reciting posies from Shakespeare, is bound to misunderstand and

distort. Such bouquet-picking leads to curiously parallel mis-
conceptions, too: Coleridge praising Shakespeare's language of
natural description in *Venus and Adonis* but missing its bawdily
comic context, and Bagehot praising Sterne's fidelity to plain
scenery and plain feeling but repudiating its context. Watkins
calls Sterne "the first real impressionist among English novelists," and others have pointed to a connection with Richardson's
mastery of immediate detail which might make him the second.
But all these estimations,[1] to be useful, ought never to lose sight
of the narrative context in which such a Wordsworthian eye for
the daisies of feeling recur. In *Tristram Shandy*, the public occasion always has a private frame.

Tristram makes his game from this classical method of narrative. Two changes signal a shift to the game sphere. He juggles
two or three of these narrative-speech progressions at the same
time. He digresses for pleasure, not from narrative need. If we
were to try, impossibly, to disentangle the narrative threads of
Tristram Shandy, we might find a narrative-speech-narrative-
speech pattern for Walter Shandy, one for Toby, perhaps one
for Yorick. Tristram's game, or part of it, is to juggle them, to let
them fall finally into a meaningful superposition, one atop the
other. Yorick must dive for a chestnut when we expect Walter to
dive for the mysteries of name-giving; Tristram must kiss the
critic's hand when the context leads us to expect him to kiss
another part of the body; Toby, amidst the birth pangs that produce Tristram headfirst, must discourse on not hurting a hair on
a fly's head. This alternation creates a Thucydidean pattern
raised to the third power. Tristram controls the interweaving.
He is no jocular Joyce, however, only pretending to trust God
for the second sentence. Behind the pretense of chaos may lie

[1] They began early. Alan B. Howes cites a Mary Rerry's praise of
Sterne's minute painting of detail—like a Dutch genre-painting—in 1789.
(*Yorick and the Critics: Sterne's Reputation in England, 1760–1868* [New
Haven, 1958], p. 108.

careful chronology, but not always a master intelligence. Process literature this novel is, vaguely realizing itself toward a termination coincident with the author's conscious intention. Sterne's preconscious voice, Tristram, confesses throughout the novel both that he really is helter-skelter and that he only seems so, that the digressions interrupt the main story, are the main story. Confessions aside, he does not proceed at random. But his consistent principle in digression and juggled narrative hardly satisfies critical expectation. Tristram does as he pleases. Yet if, as is generally recognized, his game is the novel itself, should it surprise that his playing seeks play's characteristic reward? He is not a Shandy for nothing.

II

Tristram thinks literary genre a kind of game. Inventing a new type, the song of himself, he can invent the rules for it. None others apply: "In writing what I have set about, I shall confine myself neither to his rules, nor to any man's rules that ever lived" (I, v, 8). What more natural than his choosing the rules under which he would rest most easy? He thus stipulates at the outset a relationship with his hobby different from that his Father and Uncle use. Their responses are *mechanized* by their obsessions. He intends that his shall be liberated. Questions arise. Who is Tristram's opponent? In what kind of game does one player make up such rules as he pleases, and seemingly as he goes along? His opponents can be only two: Circumstance and Us. Tristram has trouble telling his story but the trouble forms part of the story he wants to tell. "One would think," he tells us himself, "I took pleasure in running into difficulties of this kind, merely to make fresh experiments of getting out of 'em—" (VIII, vii, 545). It is so. Circumstance proves an obstruction, more often than not, of his own contriving. He represents himself as involved in a Herculean effort to *comply* with standards, to pre-

serve above all narrative and thematic continuty. A few lines
before those just quoted:

> I declare, I do not recollect any one opinion or passage of my
> life, where my understanding was more at a loss to make ends
> meet, and torture the chapter I had been writing, to the service of
> the chapter following it, than in the present case.

But the struggle really dramatized is not his compliance with
the regular rules of any one genre. He does not manfully wrestle
with Art. Instead, he dramatizes Ease warping Art to its own
particular purposes. Stedmond comes close to Tristram's real
business.

> Tristram as clown-author draws attention to the very real obsta-
> cles which lie in the path of artistic accomplishment, emphasizes
> the human frailties of even the greatest authors, and creates a
> critical awareness in the reader of some of the goals which
> authors have sought; in the process of all this he is perhaps calling
> into question the attainability of these goals, or even the desirability
> of attaining them.[2]

But this makes *Tristram Shandy* into a more ambitious critical
treatise than it is. Tristram deposes only that conventional artistic purpose is not his, that he lives not for Art but for Pleasure.
In its pursuit he scorns his second possible opponent, Us, as
much as the recalcitrant Circumstance so much supposed to in-
timidate him. Self-conscious as he is, poseur to his fingertips, still
he makes us play his game. It is a new one. We try to figure out
what the rules are. He remains to us cavalier. Follow me if you
can. His particular pleasure lies elsewhere—in himself. In this
sense the novel is *not* (*pace* Traugott) rhetorical at all. It turns
in on itself. Tristram pleases himself. His game is an *ilinx*, a
self-imposed dizziness. At this game one can play. No audience

---

[2] John M. Stedmond. *The Comic Art of Laurence Sterne* (Toronto,
1967), p. 68.

needed. The implication of this stands central to our interpretation of *Tristram Shandy*. Both Tristram and his novel are auto-erotic not rhetorical. They aim not to persuade but to please themselves. We may admire their world, but we are not asked to join it. In a limited but very real sense neither novel nor narrator cares what we think.

When Tristram seems solicitous about his reader, he has more often than not his own designs in mind. He is a man of many morals. Part of his game with the reader is to offer a constant farrago of philosophic reflection and moralizing, challenging him to take his ironic or serious pick. We are told that mirth is at the center of the universe and mocked for our grave faces. At the same time, within the unprepossessing Silenus box of jesting lurks real philosophic wisdom. We seek it out. And are mocked for that. We are damned if we do and damned if we don't. This strategy denies us a single point of view in the novel, a philosophic control as it were, and then continually alerts us to the need for one. Thus we must constantly search for a key, a basis for interpretation, and feel silly for doing so. As Burckhardt prefaces his try, "To look for the 'law' of *Tristram Shandy* is one of the least promising enterprises in criticism."[3] The strategy tells the critical history of the novel. We accept one or the other of the various morals offered—sentimentality (the Victorians), stoical humor (Stedmond, Piper), the vanity of learning (Jefferson), the artificiality of literary convention (Lehman), the vanity of words and need for fellow-feeling (Traugott), the dependability of moral sentiment and orthodox religion (Cash)—and interpret the rest of the novel as supplementary if it agrees, ironic if it does not. The sentiment was for a long time seen as pure and unalloyed but that day, I take it, is now over. When Le Fever is killed off, we weep as self-conscious, ironical weepers should. Sentiment may still be, in Toby, the book's center, but

[3] Sigurd Burckhardt, "*Tristram Shandy*'s Law of Gravity," *ELH*, XXVIII (1961).

Traugott's penetrating analysis of its rhetoric calls that and all—since it calls words—in doubt. A radical skepticism seems now the only general position and a dependence on the goodness of feeling the only path out of a vast perplexity. *157006*

The reader, then, is deliberately made uneasy, and his unease backlights Tristram's perfect ease. Tristram knows his way around in his own world perfectly. He should. He has made it to please himself. The reader's search for a key to the novel is really a search for a way to enjoy a pleasure—living in a world one *has* made, one has (Kenneth Burke's term) *earned* by a full understanding—similar to Tristram's. We may put this search into two frames of reference. We may say that the reader is offered a critical and rhetorical problem (understanding the novel) whose solution will lead to a moral awareness (the moral wisdom inside the Silenus box), a final point of view. Or we may say that the reader is offered a posture of puzzlement and discomfort. He does not know whether to laugh or cry. He must always analyze first. A point of view will make him again easy because he will once more be able to respond spontaneously. His naïveté will have been restored. If we think of Tristram's deliberate puzzlement of the reader (that is, think of *Tristram Shandy*) as Tristram's game, and of ourselves as invited to play it in order to gain the freedom and pleasure of the novel's world, do we not have an analogy with Toby's character, with the movement from absorption in game to a liberation of the feelings, a true spontaneity? We are, that is, invited to follow Toby's example. We too will be laughed at, but we will gain, in a hopefully more sophisticated way, what Toby has gained, a universe where our feelings are reliable, can be depended upon.

Thus it is a mistake, I think, to entertain the idea of fellow-feeling, social sympathy, as an external point of view brought into the novel—or even found there, internal—which will lead us out of the maze Sterne's radical discounting of language creates. It seems rather something you earn by finding your way out of the maze, penetrating the novel's rhetoric. We must understand before we can feel. What we must understand, as we see it in Yorick and the Shandy brothers, is that pleasure, satisfaction, is the necessary precondition to the kind of selfless feeling for others on which a true society—rather than merely a collection of individuals—must be based. Toby has undergone this training unaware. For us it will be self-conscious. Thus that the novel is sentimental, rather than full of sentiment, is to be expected. One of the lessons Tristram teaches us is that when we feel for others, we do so largely for the pleasure of the feeling. The Victorian objection that none of Sterne's sentiment is sincere must be very much to the point. It is in the nature of feeling, we are thus told, to be self-serving. When we are invited to observe ourselves feeling, and enjoying feeling, for other people, we are not to conclude that this is a satirical reflection on our hypocrisy. There is nothing hypocritical about taking pleasure. Furthermore, it is the necessary precondition to spontaneous feeling. Sentimentality must precede sentiment. We will feel for others only when we have felt enough for ourselves.

A great deal has been made of *Tristram Shandy* as a deliberate attempt to point out the inadequate narrative method Sterne saw in the eighteenth-century novel and to remedy it. Thus Fluchère argues:

> La digression est plus qu'une exaltante affirmation de liberté, elle devient le docile instrument de capture d'un réel malévole et fuyant, elle explore les domaines secrets de l'espace et du temps, de la connaissance et du mystère.[4]

Is it impertinent to ask what are these secrets of time and space? What are the victories of Sterne's narrative method? Apart from the penetralia of free association, how much do the digressions expand our ideas of time and space? Very little. To make Sterne

[4] Henri Fluchère, *Laurence Sterne, de l'homme à l'oeuvre* (Paris, 1961), p. 248.

a prophet of fictional technique seems equally uncalled for. If conventional form had a symbolic value for him it must have been a general one—the Censor, the Public Life's discipline. Plot equals Duty. The novel's response is Tristram's .Too coy, too concerned with dramatizing his breaking the rules, he avoids ceremoniously the discipline of form. He does it, we might add, not to philosophize about communication, though he invites us to do this, but because he enjoys it. Sir Walter Scott, we remember, had called *Tristram Shandy* "no narrative but a collection of scenes, dialogues, and portraits, humorous or affecting, intermixed with much wit, and with much learning, original or borrowed." And a modern historian of Sterne's commentators says flatly: "No one can argue sensibly that the novel is of a piece."[5] Are we not now at a point where we can admit the soundness of this view (lasting after all as it has almost from Sterne's day to this) and still see a single pattern, a unifying force and psyche, in Tristram and the kind of hobbyhorse he rides? Might we not see the struggle between philosophical self and rhetorical self *allegorized* by the struggle between conventional and "easy" narrative?

III

We might begin our discussion of Tristram's vertigo with the famous Shandean dash. It has come to represent Sterne's allegiance to a reality greater than ordinary chronological and syntactical narrative can provide. One of a graduated series of interruptions the novel offers, does it not incarnate the pleasure-principle much rather? The breakings-off, often on a scale larger than the Shandean dash comprehends, can, from Tristram's point of view, hardly be called a principle of interruption at all. They

[5] Sir Walter Scott, *Sir Walter Scott: On Novelists and Fiction*, ed. Ioan Williams (London, 1968), p. 74; Lodwick Hartley, *Laurence Sterne in the Twentieth Century* (Chapel Hill, N.C., 1966), p. 67.

keep us off balance; this, positively stated, they do for him too. He, as he says himself, continually rushes about. Not to fetch a metaphor from too far, we might call him a juggler. Centered in his poise, in his search for it, stands a fondness for keeping several things going at once. We must know him as a literary borrower, see his sources as sources, so as to relish their orchestration into his theme. (We recall Sterne's fondness for vertiginous sources, Rabelais for example.) Tristram does not make over a novel's regular components into a new vehicle for new space and time. He but juggles them. A misplaced preface, two chapters left empty to be filled later make a virtuoso point. Watch! Tristram pulls it off. He drops nothing. And a gamesman, too, we see him checking rein on the novel's other hobbies, insuring none runs away. So, too, with the vertinginous flight from Death which parades his bleeding lungs across Europe; how else does it fit the Yorkshire Epic of Shandy Hall than as part of Tristram's virtuoso display? So also Tristram's (probably we should say Sterne's) continual sensitivity to the *motions* of his own body— blood flowing, heart pounding. To the *ilinx* we can also refer his interest in gesture and in physical balance and (reaching for the left-hand pocket handkerchief with the right hand) imbalance. Finally might we not think the periodic-two-volume appearance of the novel as Tristram's attempts to regain inner balance, as an *act* (in both senses) which symbolized poise regained? From this viewpoint, all Tristram's obstacles make sense as self-induced. Such are the rules, the artificial barriers of any *ludus* with a single player. Tristram plays solitaire in a real sense, a game by himself with his life and what he thinks of it which, for his own purposes, he lets us share. We should not press Tristram's self-sufficient isolation too far. Yet, so generally received is his character as complacent stooge for his audience, the point should be made.

Tristram tells us that he will continue his regular installments until he dies. And, with perhaps an interruption,[6] it seems really to have been Sterne's design. He poses his fictional self a permanent challenge to continue, to keep up the improvising forever. Each will have his opinion on how well the later volumes answer the challenge, but the challenge itself galvanizes the book as hobby. Its failure to present a theme—for the Life and Opinions conception expands to gas before our eyes—challenges the improvisational power increasingly. Will he be able to go on? If you have no theme, no subject, you will end up like Lyly, like Nash, like Tristram, talking about yourself. Will your personality be adequate to sustain it? To control it? Again the game is an effort at balance, control. To intensify the game, Tristram not only puts the regular parts of the novel in confused motion,[7] he holds our attention on the verbal surface of the novel,[8] even on the physical components of the book, putting all these at odds to deny us a firm point of view.

Sterne's wit constituted, Traugott tells us, "a description of experience in terms of unlikely relations."[9] Surely as one such description, Tristram plays his wit on the interfaces between the prose styles he not only juggles but parodies. Without going out

---

[6] Sterne wrote in 1766 (to Edward Stanley?) that he meant to stop *Tristram Shandy* after the ninth volume and "begin a new work of four volumes, which when finish'd, I shall continue Tristram with fresh spirit." (Laurence Sterne, *Letters of Laurence Sterne*, ed. Lewis P. Curtis [Oxford, 1935], p. 284.)

[7] Look, for example, at the *motion* implied in Alan D. McKillop's description of Bobby's death: "Thus we have in the space of a few chapters concurrent actions which taken together give the impression of depth or extension, interruption and frustration, futile rhetoric, imperfect communication, surprising cause-effect sequences, unpredictable transitions and associations of ideas, trivial physical symbols for great things, and the basic idea of the machine." (*The Early Masters of English Fiction* [Lawrence, Kan., 1956], p. 200.)

[8] See Robert A. Donovan, *The Shaping Vision: Imagination in the English Novel from Defoe to Dickens* (Ithaca, N.Y., 1966), p. 90.

[9] John M. Traugott, *Tristram Shandy's World: Sterne's Philosophic Rhetoric* (Berkeley and Los Angeles, 1954), p. 28.

of bounds we might remark in passing the configuration into which Tristram's game here falls. At the center of his utterance ranges the *sermo cottidianus*, the colloquial style that is Sterne's great glory. It is, as Glaesener shrewdly observed in his 1927 *TLS* essay, a de-Latinized prose. One surrounded, we might add, by Latinized ones. It functions as stylistic control, the symbol of Tristram talking—and writing—as fast as he can—but always in imaginative control. His agility in moving from style to style, from curse to mock-heroic invocation to *Tristrapaedia*, to travel-book, to high pathos, always with his own style running through and informing the others, displays yet again his virtuoso, self-pleasing balance. In this effort to preserve its balance and complementarily destroy ours, *Tristram Shandy* much resembles some Elizabethan prose fictions, *Euphues* for example in one way, *The Unfortunate Traveller* in another.

According to Howes, Coleridge was "the first critic to recognize so clearly the sharp distinction between the humor to be found in Sterne's characters, who display a thorough knowledge of human nature, and the more questionable humor to be found in Sterne's style and manner."[10] This effort to split off Tristram from his novel came partly from misunderstanding the kind of game he plays with the reader, and more importantly with himself, but more from misapprehending Tristram the bawdy joker. To this much misunderstood role, our consideration of Tristram must now turn.

Part of the philosophizing that Sterne's comedy has undergone in recent years has been a conception of the bawdry as Shakespearean, reductive. It aims to puncture man's inflated sense of motive and self, remind him of his body. "In his use of the equivoque he is close kin to Shakespeare, most of whose jollier puns—lucky for him—are no longer understood."[11] So too,

[10] Howes, *Yorick and the Critics*, p. 116.
[11] Ernest N. Dilworth, *The Unsentimental Journey of Laurence Sterne* (New York, 1948), p. 109.

Fluchère: "Elle est donc un instrument docile entre les mains de l'auteur comique et du satiriste, qui en usent libéralement pour rabaisser par le rire l'orgueil de l'homme à des proportions raisonnables."[12] And when it is not pointing to the limitations of nature, its affair is a still more serious marking out the boundary conditions of language. "Puns and double meanings emphasize the unstable nature of language, its dynamic qualities which are so difficult to control. One can never really be sure of saying what one means."[13] (In a world so Jung and easily Freudened as that of *Tristram Shandy*, though, might it not be the other way around? You say what you really mean no matter what you say.) Instead of shocking for cheap effect, leering at the reader to make sure he gets the joke (Thackeray's old complaint), Sterne is cultivating with his reader the carefully controlled self-conscious relationship Traugott finds at the heart of *Tristram Shandy's* rhetoric. The reader is made to expose his own false pudicity, and, moving it aside, to grasp Tristram's principal topic, his sexual misfortunes. Thus the social hypocrisy surrounding sexuality is exposed and a new, more healthy decorum opened out. The method by which this is done is a broad range of equivocation, from scholarly equivalents that sterilize what they describe (*os pubis, argumentum ad rem*) to general words (nose, hornworks) bearing a particular and well-known innuendo, to very general words (thing, it) which can bear any amount of innuendo.[14]

Persuasive as this argument is, and restorative of Sterne to his proper place in the first rank of comic writers, it may mistake if not Sterne's seriousness, his *kind* of seriousness. What seems to separate Sterne's bawdry from its Shakespearean coun-

[12] Fluchère, *Laurence Sterne, de l'homme à l'oeuvre*, p. 433.
[13] Stedmond, *Comic Art*, p. 44.
[14] I am paraphrasing here William Bowman Piper's excellent discussion of "Tristram's Trial by Prudery," *Laurence Sterne* (New York, 1965), pp. 66 ff.

terpart is its fleshlessness, its manifest disinclination to arouse. As C. E. Vaughan remarks shrewdly of the bawdry in *Tristram Shandy*: "It works, as it were, in a void which he has created specially for the purpose and of which he alone, of all writers, holds the secret. In this dry handling of the matter, the affections of the reader are left unenlisted and unmoved."[15] By "void" I take him to mean context. Two of the bluest in the novel, Phutatorius with his chestnut and the Abbess of Andouillet with her novice, are also among the most revealing of Sterne's unique kind of bawdy joking.

The incident of the hot chestnut is, rather like the chestnut itself, dropped into a seemingly irrelevant parenthesis. (It begins in IV, xxiii, 302 ff.) At the beginning, Walter Shandy wonders to Yorick if Tristram's disastrously mistaken christening can be reversed; at the end, Kysarcius delivers his after-the-Visitation-Dinner paper on the subject. And in between Sterne does his best to obscure the relevance of his frame. The brothers Shandy go to the Visitation dinner in a chapter of ten pages (IV, xxiv) which Tristram has torn out of the book. Walter tells us that he hates great dinners (IV, xxiii, 302) before we know to which dinner he refers. Yorick tears up his Visitation Sermon to light pipes with before we know that he has preached it. We are in the midst of Didius's discussion of Tristram's naming blunder (IV, xxix, 326) without that previous managing of the conversation (IV, xxiii, 302) which Yorick desiderates. And when the dinner is over, Walter is "hugely tickled" with the subtleties of the disputation but, so far as we can see, no wiser than when he set out. We are invited to reassemble the scattered bones of the fruitless errand around the dramatic interlude that "Zounds!" introduces, the only part of the parenthesis narrated in ordinary chronological time.

The loose strands are manifestly there to reweave, of course.

---

[15] C. E. Vaughan, "Sterne and the Novel of His Times," *Cambridge History of English Literature*, X (Cambridge, 1913), 51–74.

The indecorum in Phutatorius's breech breaches the social decorum of the whole company. Indecorum of another sort has been on Tristram's mind. It was why he left out Chapter XXIV:

—But the painting of this journey, upon reviewing it, appears to be so much above the stile and manner of any thing else I have been able to paint in this book, that it could not have remained in it, without depreciating every other scene; and destroying at the same time that necessary equipoise and balance, (whether of good or bad) betwixt chapter and chapter, from whence the just proportions and harmony of the whole work results. [IV, xxv, 315]

We are thus to add to our sense of the chestnut's social, a sense of its literary, indecorum. And, as is often the case with Sterne, his insistence on its being out of place invites us to redefine the scene until it has a place. To this theme of indecorum we are thus made aware of, we must add another, the uses of eloquence. Yorick puts his sermon to use by tearing it up into tapers. And after the interruption, Phutatorius is counseled to put a sheet or two of his own recently reprinted *de Concubinis retinendis* to use as a fomentive dressing for his scorched *membrum virile*. Sandwiched between these two illustrative incidents we have an example of true eloquence, one that does indeed mock both Yorick's eloquence which has preceded and Kysarcius's which is to follow. "Zounds!" It interrupts Yorick's depreciation of his own candied utterance:

I have undergone such unspeakable torments, in bringing forth this sermon, quoth *Yorick*, upon this occasion,—that I declare, *Didius*, I would suffer martyrdom—and if it was possible my horse with me, a thousand times over, before I would sit down and make such another: I was delivered of it at the wrong end of me—it came from my head instead of my heart—and it is for the pain it gave me, both in the writing and preaching of it, that I revenge myself of it, in this manner.—To preach, to shew the

extent of our reading, or the subtleties of our wit—to parade it
in the eyes of the vulgar with the beggarly accounts of a little
learning, tinseled over with a few words which glitter, but con-
vey little light and less warmth—is a dishonest use of the poor
single half hour in a week which is put into our hands—'Tis not
preaching the gospel—but ourselves—For my own part, continued
Yorick, I had rather direct five words point blank to the heart—.
[IV, xxvi, 317]

It also deflates it. Not even five words are needed. When unspeakable torment really fathers eloquence, one will do. Tristram
interrupts this interruption to quash Toby, brought to his feet
by "point blank," and to alert us to still another kind of indecorum, this time religious.

—when a single word, and no more, uttered from the opposite
side of the table, drew every one's ears towards it—a word of all
others in the dictionary the last in that place to be expected—a
word I am ashamed to write—yet must be written—must be
read;—illegal—uncanonical—guess ten thousand guesses, multi-
plied into themselves—rack—torture your invention for ever,
you're where you was—In short, I'll tell it in the next chapter.
[IV, xxvi, 317–318]

Tristram protests too much, of course. Zounds was not precisely
God's Wounds, even on such an occasion. But the rhetorical
climax is thus properly and fully built. Indecorum and Eloquence come together in a word. The explosion occurs on carefully prepared thematic ground.

Sterne has reinforced this thematic structure with some resolute punning that yokes together decorous and indecorous scene,
true and false eloquence. Amid the canonical transactions and
the port, for example, Phutatorius's "whole thoughts and attention were taken up with a transaction which was going forwards
at that very instant within the precincts of his own *Galligaskins*,
and in a part of them, where of all others he stood most inter-

ested to watch accidents" (IV, xxvii, 319). Within the Cathedral precinct, then, we have another kind of precinct altogether, and in place of an accident of the logical sort (something inessential to the conception of an object—a good many float around this dinner table) quite another kind. When the deplorable accident happens, the metaphor chosen to describe it puns on the physical manner of the accident: "it so fell out, however, that one was actually sent rolling off the table" (IV, xxvii, 320). Tristram begins a pun on "door" when he describes what the chestnut fell into: "—let it suffice to say—it was that particular aperture, which in all good societies, the laws of decorum do strictly require, like the temple of *Janus* (in peace at least) to be universally shut up."

Whether or not it was, like the temple of Janus, far more open than shut, we are not told. It seems likely, however, that we are to extend the comparison in a bawdy way. Phutatorius's breeches, like the temple doors, are closed in peace but opened for war. "The neglect of this punctilio," a cliché we are invited to literalize tells us, "had opened a door to this accident." From accident as sudden misfortune, Tristram turns to philosophic accident, uncaused occurrence. It may have a meaning, after all, and one related to Phutatorius's treatise *de Concubinis retinendis.* We are meant to keep this in mind until, when Yorick owns to a sin he did not commit, the episode's discussion of accident becomes fully clear. Meanwhile, Tristram's use of the accidents of language continues. The gap in Phutatorius's breeches, to Tristram—as a historian determined not to dip *his* pen in the controversy—resembles a gap in a manuscript account, a "hiatus." A literally apt cliché once again tells us that "Phutatorius was not able to dive into the secret of what was going forwards below." And when Yorick picks up the chestnut Phutatorius has flung down, the injured party takes so irrevocable a conviction that he looks on his injurer "that *Euclid's* demonstrations, could they be brought to batter it in breach [the exclamation, we should recall Tristram telling us, was definitely not canonical], should not all have power to overthrow it." And the soul of the jest is explained when we see the literal "chucking the chestnut hot into *Phutatorius's* ****" become "a sarcastical fling at his book." A book, we are again reminded with a pun, which "had inflamed many an honest man in the same place." Thus the "master-stroke of arch-wit" becomes literally as well as figuratively a stroke. Yorick, however, was not guilty of it, we are almost-assuredly told. His sense of humor was too "tempered" to make it hot for an enemy in this way. But he will not stoop to explain why he stooped for the chestnut ("he could not stoop to tell his story to them"). He thus takes the rap for casting the chestnut into the aperture: "This heroic cast produced him inconveniences in many respects." Cast of mind and cast of hand become one. The mental and the physical thus wordplayfully conflated come together most heroically when Phutatorius's injury is treated by the sanative particles floating on a page from his own book, hot, or rather cool, off the press from round the corner. The scene reminds one of the Wife of Bath, tearing from Janekyn's book the leaves that describe her own literary ancestry, the leaves from which she has been created. Literal and imaginative reality are, for comic effect, brought to the same level. Just as Yorick's sermon fires his listeners by lighting their pipes, Phutatorius finds his book "best to take out the fire" of the chestnut.

The reader ought not fear, in such a universe of bawdy convertibility, that he will read *in sensu obscaeno* what was innocently meant. A calculated synergism of innuendo, in fact, invites him to look for—and find—bawdry everywhere. It is tempting to see in this surface pattern of wordplay a manifestation of that ineluctable human physicality that the chestnut's genial warmth asserts with more drama. Low and high come yoked together only, and Sterne can pivot on a pun from one to the other; the bawdry makes an essentially philosophical statement.

Tempting but, I think, finally wrong. For the presiding deity of Sterne's wordplay is not Truth but Ease. The butt of the joke, after all, is Phutatorius. No one has accused him of neglecting the flesh. He needs no Mercutio in his garden. Nor does Walter Shandy, whose philosophy *includes* the Ass Kicking. Nor Tristram, who tells us in a pun (IV, xxv, 314) that the sinister turn of his own and all the Shandys' lives, has come from that bend sinister on the coach. Nor does any Petrarchan gush need ventilation. The pattern of punning, like the wordplay of other sorts, leads nowhere outside the context of the scene itself. It aims only to make us comfortable within it. It caters to a mind on vacation from philosophy, a mind at play. The innuendo doubtless must be classed as false wit, fancy rather than judgment, scheme rather than trope. Yet few can have wondered, with a *bawdy* pun, "by what perverseness of industry" *it* was ever found. The sense of endless connection may be a device of low wit but it is infinitely reassuring. Once used to it, we follow Sterne's transitions with ease, cease to worry over the narrative discontinuities. We are no longer in a world we never made and no longer, therefore, worry about that world's unfathomability. Rather than probing the infinite undependability of language from a philosophical point of view, Sterne is demonstrating how it can become a dependable, pleasure-giving thing to man—from an imaginative point of view. Sterne finds it, in fact, one of man's great weapons *against* chance as well as being expressive of it. Undependable, not to trust, language certainly is. But in this passage Tristram turns the proposition around. Language helps us get something back from the deceiving universe. It goes far, in this episode, toward creating a comic fitness that counterstates the social and literary indecorum. By this means, Sterne offers, not a grin-and-bear-it comic stoicism but an assertive, free-swinging comic world where justice works with joyful gusto. A new kind of eloquence (traditional, though, in its combining of word and gesture into convincing *ethos*) and a new kind of

decorum emerge from the scene, from the careful structure leading up to, and surrounding, "Zounds!"

The principal actor in the scene is not Phutatorius but Yorick.
He both creates the scene's comedy and defines it. In the epi-
gram from *Encheiridion* V which stood on the title page of
Volumes I and II,[16] Sterne gives fair warning of a concentration
on attitude rather than event. And when the event stands out
as really crucial, it tends to disappear altogether. So it is here.
We are led to believe, but not all the way to belief, that Yorick
did not drop the hot chestnut into Phutatorius's breeches. It
seems that he did not, but it would have been very like him to
do so. Why not let him father the joke? Would it be any the less
funny if he had nudged the chestnut? It seems so. What Yorick
does, finally, is capitalize on chance. If we follow Sterne's lead
that the falling-in was accidental, we should not follow it that
the picking-up was innocent. If Yorick does not pull the prank,
at least he does not deny it. And by refusing to deny it, he really
allows the joke to take place. The burn is false wit, Hazlitt's
second level of the three levels of the laughable.[17] It is Freud's
lower level, the harmless rather than the tendentious joke.[18] By

---

[16] "It is not actions, but opinions concerning actions, which disturb men."

[17] "The essence of the laughable then is the incongruous, the disconnec-
ting one idea from another, or the jostling of one feeling against another.
. . . The accidental contradiction between our expectations and the event
can hardly be said, however, to amount to the ludicrous: it is merely
laughable. The ludicrous is where there is the same contradiction between
the object and our expectations, heightened by some deformity or incon-
venience, that is, by its being contrary to what is customary or desirable....
The third sort, or the ridiculous arising out of absurdity as well as im-
probability, that is, where the defect or weakness is of a man's own seeking,
is the most refined of all, but not always so pleasant as the last, because
the same contempt and disapprobation which sharpens and subtilises our
sense of the impropriety, adds a severity to it inconsistent with perfect
ease and enjoyment. This last species is properly the province of satire."
(William Hazlitt, *Lectures on the Comic Writers,* I–"On Wit and Humour,"
The Collected Works of William Hazlitt, ed. A. R. Waller and Arnold
Glover [London, 1903], VIII, 7–8.)

[18] The whole passage, in a way, rehearses the development of the joke
as Freud describes it in *Jokes and Their Relation to the Unconscious* (trans.

taking credit for the event, lending chance a human (and aggressive) motive, connecting Phutatorius's sins with, and philosophizing about, the member receiving the injury, Yorick performs his role as jester. By stooping to pick up the chestnut, he gives sense to chance, domesticates it, makes use of it to restore an ethical balance, both for Phutatorius individually and for the whole company and its exalted speculations. He performs, that is, on the narrative level the role the wordplay performs on the literal—or imagistic—level. He takes a chance event (a hot chestnut falls where it ought to; two words share a same, comically appropriate—with, hence, its degree of "ought-to-"—sense) and capitalizes on its accidental humor to make wit. Yorick, then, teaches us what to do with chance. Capitalize on it for purposes of jest. The incident through which he does it thus becomes clearly related to this context. The brothers Shandy go to the dinner to find out what they can do about the

---

James Strachey, 2d ed., [New York, 1960], pp. 137–138): "We are now able to state the formula for the mode of operation of tendentious jokes. They put themselves at the service of purposes in order that, by means of using the pleasure from jokes as a fore-pleasure, they may produce new pleasure by lifting suppressions and repressions. . . . The joke . . . from its beginning to its perfecting . . . remains true to its essential nature. It begins as play, in order to derive pleasure from the free use of words and thoughts. As soon as the strengthening of reasoning puts an end to this play with words as being senseless, and with thoughts as being nonsensical, it changes into a jest, in order that it may retain these sources of pleasure and be able to achieve fresh pleasure from the liberation of nonsense. Next, as a joke proper, but still a non-tendentious one, it gives its assistance to thoughts and strengthens them against the challenge of critical judgement, a process in which the 'principle of confusion of sources of pleasure' is of use to it. And finally it comes to the help of major purposes which are combating suppression, in order to lift their internal inhibitions by the 'principle of fore-pleasure.' Reason, critical judgement, suppression—these are the forces against which it fights in succession; it holds fast to the original sources of verbal pleasure and, from the stage of the jest onwards, opens new sources of pleasure for itself by lifting inhibitions. The pleasure that it produces, whether it is pleasure in play or pleasure in lifting inhibitions, can invariably be traced back to economy in psychical expenditure, provided that this view does not contradict the essential nature of pleasure and that it proves itself fruitful in other directions."

terrible name chance has given Tristram. They are not the wiser for it, but Tristram clearly is. For his name stands for the peculiar fate life has given him and capitalizing on this fate for comic purposes is precisely what he is doing in this episode and throughout *Tristram Shandy*.[19] From a knight of sadness he must, through his book, become a knight of joy. He must renounce his name. Thus the narrative level of the episode becomes an allegory of the relation between true and false wit. Real accident causes the one; true wit is created when accident becomes, is made to become, expressive of man's purpose.

There is, then, a lesson of wit to be learned here as well as one in—as Sterne lets us know in plain words—"How finely we argue upon mistaken facts" (IV, xxvii, 319). This second has been often pointed out. Walter Shandy again philosophizes in excess of the stimulus. But if we may for a moment play the simpleminded reader of satire, what would we have him reason? "Merciful Heavens! There goes another one of those hot chestnuts! Will Phutatorius never learn?" Walter is set up here to be put down so that we do not notice Tristram using essentially the same device, a high style for a low subject, an apparatus and nomenclature of learning to describe a scene for which, also, "there is no chaste word throughout all Johnson's dictionary." The tradition of learned wit has for a long time been recognized in Sterne,[20] but Walter's function as lightning rod for it seems less familiar. The juxtaposition is one between an unaware comic disproportion of style and subject (Walter Shandy's) and an aware one (Tristram's, and ours). Here, too, the structure of the bawdry seems to suggest a difference between true wit and false. Sterne does not seem to be saying that "Zounds" and the mistaken responses it provokes show, really, how finely we argue

[19] See, in this connection, Piper's discussion of the role of chance in the novel, *Laurence Sterne*, pp. 49–51.
[20] D. W. Jefferson, *"Tristram Shandy* and the tradition of Learned Wit," *Essays in Criticism*, I (1951), 225–248.

on mistaken facts. For we see the company arguing really finely on a mistaken fact when they hold Yorick guilty for tipping in the chestnut. Both judgments, so far as we know (alas, Poor Locke), are factually mistaken, but one is much truer than the other. One makes beautiful comic sense, the other poor serious sense. We are asked to choose to look at life comically and, so far as things have meaning for men, meaningfully, or to look at life seriously and mistakenly. Sterne aims to point, that is, a difference not only between true wit and false but between wit and judgment, between seeing differences and seeing resemblances.

Why, one might ask, this particular chance? Sterne seems to suggest an explanation when he makes Yorick's stooping for the chestnut echo Othello's familiar falling for the handkerchief.

> It is curious to observe the triumph of slight incidents over the mind:—What incredible weight they have in forming and governing our opinions, both of men and things,—that trifles light as air, shall waft a belief into the soul, and plant it so immoveably within it. [IV, xxvii, 322]

Iago says of his trap for Othello:

> I will in Cassio's lodging lose this napkin,
> And let him find it. Trifles light as air
> Are to the jealous confirmations strong
> As proofs of holy writ.   [III, iii]

This is the particular chance which character has prepared for, which we can turn to our own purposes. No good at reasoning, we are better at opportunism. The contrast here (comedy makes sense of one accident—Zounds—while serious philosophy fails with another—Tristram instead of Trismegistus) looks very like that between the *Knight's Tale* and the *Miller's Tale*. The moral would seem to be the same. Sharp-eyed living will do more for you—Dr. Johnson kicking the stone to refute Berkeley—than formal ratiocination. Chance and character are likely to lend to a meaningless world a meaningful pattern. If we do not know what to ask for, still we get what we deserve. This trusting to chance fits nicely with Tristram's professed method of composition, which trusts to a higher but nearly as inscrutable power.[21]

The incident of the chestnut, then, itself provides the answer to the question of the narrative parenthesis that encloses it: What do you do if by chance you have been named, as it were, sadly? You establish a comic decorum, a comic justice. You make a joke because a joke makes sense of the world. Yet all this does not add up to a philosophical bawdry. For the bawdry is there, like the rest of the highly conceited rhetorical structure, to educate the reader only in how to get pleasure. If we must call it philosophical, it is Hedonistic, not comically Stoic. Sterne gets down in the bawdy ditch not to philosophize on what a piece of mixed work is man but because that is where the jokes are. It is Sterne's dirty joking that has kept alive his much discussed learned wit. If we come to the day when sexuality is as public as eating, *Tristram Shandy* will be as dead as *Euphues*. So will Rabelais, who pinned his learned comedy to the same star.

If, with the chestnut, Sterne dramatized the role of the jester, in the affair of the Abbess of Andouillets and her novice he illustrates the role of the jest. The narrative parenthesis is wedged into a context of swift coach travel. It begins with Tristram going on at a tearing rate toward Fontainebleau:

> Still—still I must away—the roads are paved—the posts are short—the days are long—'tis no more than noon—I shall be at *Fontainbleau* before the king. [VII, xix, 502]

And when it ends shortly after, he is still on the way:

---

[21] It fits, too, and nicely indeed the play whence Yorick fetches his name. For Hamlet has a plan no more than Tristram, plays a desperate opportunism (what else can he mean by "Let be?") and, like Yorick, gets credit for a revenge chance puts in his way.

What a tract of country have I run! [VII, xxvi, 510]

And, in the next sentence and chapter, he has arrived at Andouillets and is describing it. The episode thus sandwiched is
appropriately enough about getting on. It is a blue one indeed.
The Abbess comes on stage in a syntactical confusion that ren-
ders her part of the geography of Burgundy and Savoy as well
as part of the history of European muscular therapy, all in a
single sentence:

> The abbess of *Andouillets,* which if you look into the large set of
> provincial maps now publishing at *Paris,* you will find situated
> amongst the hills which divide *Burgundy* from *Savoy,* being in
> danger of an *Anchylosis* or stiff joint (the *sinovia* of her knee
> becoming hard by long matins) and having tried every remedy
> ——first, prayers and thanksgiving; then invocations to all the
> saints in heaven promiscuously—then particularly to every saint
> who had ever had a stiff leg before her—then touching it with all
> the reliques of the convent, principally with the thigh-bone of
> the man of *Lystra,* who had been impotent from his youth—then
> wrapping it up in her veil when she went to bed—then cross-wise
> her rosary—then bringing in to her aid the secular arm, and
> anointing it with oils and hot fat of animals—then treating it
> with emollient and resolving fomentations——then with poultices
> of marsh-mallows, mallows, bonus Henricus, white lillies and
> fenugreek—then taking the woods, I mean the smoak of 'em,
> holding her scapulary across her lap—then decoctions of wild
> chicory, water cresses, chervil, sweet cecily and cochlearia—and
> nothing all this while answering, was prevailed on at last to try
> the hot baths of *Bourbon*—so having first obtain'd leave of the
> visitor-general to take care of her existence—she ordered all to
> be got ready for her journey: a novice of the convent of about
> seventeen, who had been troubled with a whitloe in her middle
> finger, by sticking it constantly into the abbess's cast poultices,
> &c.—had gained such an interest, that overlooking a sciatical old
> nun, who might have been set up for ever by the hot baths of

Bourbon, Margarita, the little novice, was elected as the companion of the journey. [VII, xxi, 504–505]

Everything in the passage arouses our suspicion—stiff joints, hard knee, long matins, remedy, prayers, invocations, the thighbone of the man of *Lystra,* the secular arm, all the healing nostrums (Heaven knows the key to them), the poor novice's middle finger. And it may be that we get the general outline of the relationship involved. If so, it is hard to see how its bawdiness can be philosophized. Part of man's necessary awareness of his physical self? Not exactly. Part of a satire on the hypocrisy of society in insisting that such a natural relationship be hidden? This does not seem quite what Tristram has in mind. A satire on the Church? Again, nothing in the passage indicates it. To what end, then does the bawdry tend? Perhaps the very surplus of innuendo indicates what the narrator is about. For much of the innuendo really points in vain to a bawdy equivalent. It really makes no sense that the *Abbess* has the stiff leg, or has a name that puns on little sausages. And all the funny-enough treatments for this irrelevantly suggested male member lead nowhere. If a stiff joint represents what she wants, why is the whole elaborate catachresis organized around the *healing* of the stiff joint? Unless, very perhaps, the healing represents an act of intercourse, the particular cure for a stiff joint which the Abbess seems most to desire. But, one might reply, this is not a metaphysical poem. The innuendo was not meant to withstand this kind of analysis. This is precisely the point. It is infinitely, but very vaguely, suggestive. One cannot build upon it a philosophical justification of the life of the flesh. The language does not yoke spirit and flesh together in a resigned yet hopeful Stoic vision. It yokes them together merely for the fun of playing with words. Look, for example, at the opening three and a half lines, where, by a mistaken pronoun reference, the Abbess is confused with the territory in which she resides. Shakespeare does much the same thing in *Venus and Adonis* when Venus compares her-

self to a richly landscaped park and Adonis to a deer invited
to sport therein.

> "Fondling," she saith, "since I have hemmed thee here
> Within the circuit of this ivory pale,
> I'll be a park, and thou shalt be my deer:
> Feed where thou wilt, on mountain or in dale;
>   Graze on my lips; and if those hills be dry,
>   Stray lower, where the pleasant fountains lie.
> "Within this limit is relief enough,
> Sweet bottom-grass, and high delightful plain,
> Round rising hillocks, brakes obscure and rough,
> To shelter thee from tempest and from rain.
>   Then be my deer, since I am such a park.
>   No dog shall rouse thee, though a thousand bark."
>
>   [lines 229–240]

The same thing but not at all the same kind of thing. The wit,
for Shakespeare, comes from the, as who should say, extensive
firmness of his comparison. The earthy *effictio* is spelled out—
and relevant—to the last detail. Sterne's comparison, so far as I
can see, is relevant to nothing at all. Its basis is not intellectual
correspondence but the ease of irrational comparison. If the
pronoun reference is a plain mistake, so much the better. For
the whole passage appeals to a deliberately unintellectual easi-
ness of bawdy convertibility. Once one sets up an environment
of bawdy equivalency like this, anything goes. Surely this is
precisely why Tristram sets it up. Sexual word play is more
pleasurable than any other kind because it releases the rational
censor on the meaning of words more fully than any other kind.
They are free, in this kind of context, truly to mean whatever we
want them to mean. The sexuality is not so important as freedom
from the censor. Thus we see, I think, the reason for the curious
fleshlessness of Tristram's innuendo. His aim is not sexual titilla-
tion but primal, childlike verbal pleasure, and the first is primarily the means to the second. In the freedom that such an

indefinitely encouraged punning engenders, we can see the peculiar nature of Tristram's context, of the void in which his bawdy joking takes place.

The passage aims initially then at giving us pleasure, not equipping us with a Stoic resignation. It is true that Tristram invites an indirect moral response by directing our attention to what Piper calls his trial by prudery: he must tell us what two words will make a French post-horse go and these two words are unmentionable in polite company. He makes a great fuss about this, telling us first that:

> Now as these words cost nothing, I long from my soul to tell the reader what they are; but here is the question—they must be told him plainly, and with the most distinct articulation, or it will answer no end—and yet to do it in that plain way—though their reverences may laugh at it in the bed-chamber—full well I wot, they will abuse it in the parlour: for which cause, I have been volving and revolving in my fancy some time, but to no purpose, by what clean device or facete contrivance, I might so modulate them, that whilst I satisfy *that ear* which the reader chuses to *lend* me—I might not dissatisfy the other which he keeps to himself. [VII, xx, 503]

His fingers burn to try, he tells us. And later, in the high style, just before the verbal consummation: "—and how to tell them—Ye, who can speak of every thing existing, with unpolluted lips —instruct me—guide me—" (VII, xxiv, 509). No one makes so much of contravening convention if he really wants to preserve it, and if he is making an ironic gain at the reader's expense in destroying it, I fail to see what that gain is. What he is really doing is setting up a series of artificial obstacles to the saying of the two words, so that our pleasure, when we hear them, will be that much the greater. Far from mocking the reader's false modesty (his two artificially separated ears) Tristram takes pains to *erect* precisely this false modesty where none stood before. And, again, his pleasure is not in decorum per se but in the pleasure to be gained from wittily destroying it.

The destruction comes in solving the Abbess's problem. Her mules will not get on. The prospect generates a brief passage of innuendo in which the wish fathers the thought.

> We are ruin'd and undone, my child, said the abbess to *Margarita* —we shall be here all night—we shall be plunder'd—we shall be ravish'd—
>
> —We shall be ravish'd, said *Margarita*, as sure as a gun.
>
> *Sancta Maria!* cried the abbess (forgetting the *O!*)—why was I govern'd by this wicked stiff joint? why did I leave the convent of *Andouillets?* and why didst thou not suffer thy servant to go unpolluted to her tomb?
>
> O my finger! my finger! cried the novice, catching fire at the word *servant*—why was I not content to put it here, or there, any where rather than be in this strait?
>
> —Strait! said the abbess.
>
> Strait—said the novice; for terrour had struck their understandings—the one knew not what she said—the other what she answer'd.
>
> O my virginity! virginity; cried the abbess.
>
> —inity! —inity! said the novice, sobbing. [VII, xxii, 508]

The intercourse thus promisingly begun is interrupted by the need to get the mules moving and then resumed in a verbal model for sexual intercourse which solves the nun's problems— how to say these two words politely, get going, and satisfy their sexual frustrations—and Tristram's as well:

> All sins whatever, quoth the abbess, turning casuist in the distress they were under, are held by the confessor of our convent to be either mortal or venial: there is no further division. Now a venial sin being the slightest and least of all sins,—being halved—by taking, either only the half of it, and leaving the rest—or, by taking it all, and amicably halving it betwixt yourself and another person—in course becomes diluted into no sin at all.

Now I see no sin in saying, *bou, bou, bou, bou, bou,* a hundred times together; nor is there any turpitude in pronouncing the syllable *ger, ger, ger, ger, ger,* were it from our matins to our vespers: Therefore, my dear daughter, continued the abbess of *Andouillets*—I will say *bou,* and thou shalt say *ger*; and then alternately, as there is no more sin in *fou* than in *bou*—Thou shalt say *fou*—and I will come in (like fa, sol, la, re, mi, ut, at our complines) with *ter.* And accordingly the abbess, giving the pitch note, set off thus:

Abbess, Bou——bou——bou
Margarita, —ger, ——ger, ——ger
Margarita, Fou——fou——fou
Abbess, —ter, ——ter, ——ter.

The two mules acknowledged the notes by a mutual lash of their tails; but it went no further.—'Twill answer by an' by, said the novice.

Abbess, Bou- bou- bou- bou- bou- bou-
Margarita, —ger, ger, ger, ger, ger, ger.

Quicker still, cried *Margarita.*

Fou, fou, fou, fou, fou, fou, fou, fou, fou.

Quicker still, cried *Margarita.*

Bou, bou, bou, bou, bou, bou, bou, bou, bou.

Quicker still—God preserve me! said the abbess—They do not understand us, cried *Margarita*—But the Devil does, said the abbess of *Andouillets.*

The function of the jest here lies in its sudden and simultaneous solving of all these problems by a verbal device. The formula of verbal complementation devised can stand, I think, as a model for the function of the jest. It gets us out of uncomfortable and otherwise unsolvable situations in a pleasurable way. Embarrassment orchestrates into duet. That Tristram has *made up* most of the barriers over which the joke triumphs says no more than that he has authored the joke. That we cooperate in thus consenting to put on stage a false modesty few of us (it is part of the novelist's relation with the reader's private self) really possess, is simply to say that we are the willing audience all jokes require. Here again we should stress not the undependability of words but quite the reverse. They are infinitely serviceable, the indispensable buffer between man's insatiable desire and unyielding circumstance. They help us get on and enjoy getting on. It is no accident that the episode is preceded by a "chance" allusion to the word "gay" and "spleen" and is followed by puns on slow-rising (VII, xxvii, 514), Saint *Optat*, and finally the famous reference to what, garters in hand, he did *not* do with Jenny, and the rubric VEXATION upon VEXATION (VII, xxx, 518–519). Tristram is determined to preserve his gust for joy midst the anguish of his sexual frustrations, and his chief mechanism for so doing is precisely a joke like this, in which language, rather than sublimating, *substitutes for* sexual satisfaction.

It is a mistake, I think, to apply to a passage like this the canons of Augustan wit. It is false wit that reigns, no doubt, one made up of superficial schemes. Yet the intellectual criteria that Johnson applies to Cowley, for example, precisely misfit this occasion. Tristram is not trying to satisfy the standards of intellectual connection and consistency but to evade them. Logically, there is no solution to any of the problems. Tristram does not clarify a problem, as a metaphysical poet would do. He dodges it. Watkins compares Sterne to the metaphysicals: "Undoubtedly Sterne frequently indulges in equivocation for its own sake, like the metaphysicals in their conceits."[22] In their elaboration, Sterne's conceits may resemble those of the metaphysicals, but the force of his wit seems to move in an opposite direction. Sterne aims, or at least Tristram aims, not at coherence but at pleasure. "That wit is the most refined and effectual," Hazlitt

[22] W. B. C. Watkins, *Perilous Balance* (Princeton, 1939), p. 124.

tells us, "which is founded on the detection of unexpected likeness or distinction in things, rather than in words."[23] But what if,
as here, words make the mules go better than corn? What if, as
with Tristram, words are things? In a sense, then, the Victorians
were right about Tristram's sexual innuendo. It *is* for its own
sake. It *does* come more from the head than the heart. High
seriousness cannot redeem it. Once again the Victorian objection isolates the central issue, Tristram's final loyalty to pleasure.
The infinitely manipulable world of punning exists not to
teach us a lesson but to put Tristram, with all his deficiencies,
at ease.

In the "Poetic Categories" chapter of *Attitudes Toward History*, Kenneth Burke draws a pertinent distinction between burlesque and satire.

> The writer of burlesque makes no attempt to get inside the
> psyche of his victim. Instead, he is content to select the externals
> of behavior, driving them to a "logical conclusion" that becomes
> their "reduction to absurdity." By program, he obliterates his
> victim's discriminations. He is "heartless." He converts every
> "perhaps" into a "positively." He deliberately suppresses any
> consideration of the "mitigating circumstances" that would put
> his subject in a better light. . . . Hilariously, he converts a manner
> into a mannerism. The method of burlesque (polemic, carica-
> ture) is partial not only in the sense of *partisan*, but also in the
> sense of *incompleteness*. As such, it does not contain a well-
> rounded frame within itself; we can use it for the ends of wisdom
> only insofar as we ourselves provide the ways of making allow-
> ances for it; we must not be merely *equal* to it, we must be
> enough *greater than* it to be able to "discount" what it says. [pp.
> 54–55]

Though often using the methods of burlesque, Sterne ranks in
these terms a satirist. But, we frequently learn, his satire is

[23] Hazlitt, *Lectures on the Comic Writers:* I–"On Wit and Humour,"
p. 22.

peculiarly gentle. We can now see why. Tristram supplies a central frame of reference, the games of pleasure; we can see, if he takes a swipe at Locke, just why he does it. But the satire, because of its game matrix, can never toughen: the *object* is not to attack the victim but to amuse Tristram. Tristram, if a satirist, is a self-serving one. To such an attacker, every victim is an additional source, not of rage and exasperation, but of pleasure. When someone lurks, immune to such use, just outside the game sphere, as with Mrs. Shandy (with, Tristram tells us, all the other Shandy women), no pleasure comes from the attack and it turns dull and flaccid. Such people, and only such, cannot bask in the novel's genial tolerance of private amusement. They seem scarcely alive. The standards for life, those that supply satiric point of view, are the standards of game. The only character who really meets them (alone in his self-consciousness about motive) acknowledges to himself that his motive is pleasure. We readers class ourselves as equals or victims, depending on our willingness to recognize this essential motive in him, the tale he tells, and ourselves.

We have perhaps ignored ourselves, ignored Tristram's audience. Of course he is an actor, harrows his resources of feeling to benefit the audience.[24] And he keeps his eye continually on it. But its demands, like all others, he just as continually tries to avoid, dramatizes his trying to avoid. His relation to us is like his relation to everything else. What fun can be gotten from us? Critics find Tristram's, and the novel's, relation to audience a pretty metaphysical matter. Fluchère, for example:

> C'est un aveu implicite que le livre n'existe pas en soi, dans l'impersonnalité indifférente de l'oeuvre d'art, mais qu'il recevra son sens et pourra remplir sa fonction d'après l'accueil qui lui sera fait.[25]

---

[24] See Martin Price, *To the Palace of Wisdom* (New York, 1964), p. 337, for a fine statement of this case.

[25] Fluchère, *Laurence Sterne, de l'homme à l'oeuvre*, p. 235.

In this view, we function as audience by restoring to narrative and spiritual coherence Tristram's skillful chaos. He digs the hole; we fill it up. But this spoils the game! Misapprehends what Tristram is doing! He invites us to search for the center of the Silenus box but, as with Rabelais, from this center emerges, not the stern voice of coherence, but the Abbey of Thélème. *Fay ce que vouldras.* To try putting the pieces together, is to become audience for the *Sermons*, not *Tristram Shandy*, become one of the satirized. Surely our role points rather to admiring Tristram's performance than to weeping for a world where such desperate enactments need to take place. We should admire him not for his success in reenacting the blooming and buzzing confusion of an absurd world but for his success, as a precocious child in the gardcn of Western culture, in pleasing himself. The narrative structure of *Tristram Shandy* imitates his play: the pleasure-principle at work on the principles of narrative itself.

How shall we criticize, appraise such a structure? The standards of "process literature" Northrop Frye has pointed out[26] as very different from those for the finished, balanced, classical creation. How does this difference apply to Tristram Shandy?

> The question of structure in *Tristram Shandy* may be discussed, I think, without reference to the question of whether the novel is a finished whole, for what we need to know is not whether the book might have been continued, or even whether it reaches a stable point of rest, but what principle, if any, controls its seemingly erratic and aimless progression.[27]

If we can agree that Tristram's *ilinx*, his dizzying pursuit of pleasure, provides such a center, where do we stand? How can such an artifact be criticized? The easy answer simply asks, "Did you enjoy it?" In other words, *Tristram Shandy's* critical reputation

[26] Northrop Frye, "Toward Defining an Age of Sensibility," in *Eighteenth Century English Literature*, ed. James L. Clifford (New York, 1959).

[27] Donovan, *The Shaping Vision*, pp. 113–114.

answers our question. It worked. Tristram won. Sterne won. The book sold. No negligible reply this. Tristram's concern for sales is *in* the book. Sterne's concern for fame is *in* the *Letters,* in everything he ever wrote. *Tristram Shandy* is improvisational, one of those seminal books about nothing in particular, a rhetorical gesture for fame. The reader's central role in the novel is to buy it. The book's major function is to sell. These categories, crass and simpleminded, fit the novel well. There has been a great fuss about the genre of *Tristram Shandy.*[28] Surely part of its *ludus* is farce, a great expandable skin stuffed (enfarced) with a mishmash that pleased Sterne and Sterne thought would please. The book is full of topical appeals.[29] "Of course the sentimental setpieces are there to be enjoyed," we might surprise the old joker in saying. "What else are they for, Pray?" No small part of the book's power—and critical reputation—comes from palming off these period-piece rehearsals so well. After all, we know what self-conscious sentiment, what sentimentality is because of Sterne.

But a document does not join the immortals by incidental appeal, however well honed. If, like the Victorians, we find little else, then let "historical interest" describe it. The modern view sees the novel philosophizing about communication, about language. Tristram is a loser, an antihero, doomed to failure but bracing up. Reading the novel as we have we must emphasize instead Tristram's success. He pleases us. He pleases himself. And he can do the first because he has done the second. His interest for us will lie precisely in the revelation his game makes about the nature of all games and, more largely, of all human motive. They return, finally, to pleasure. They cherish no theme beyond it. They are ends in themselves. "True play," as Huizinga

[28] See Hartley's amusing collection of conjectures (*Laurence Sterne in the Twentieth Century,* p. 22).

[29] Not in the narrow sense. Sterne rightfully boasted to Dodsley that he had gotten all the local detail out of the book.

says, "knows no propaganda; its aim is in itself, and its familiar spirit is happy inspiration."

One perennial perplexity remains to plague us. When do we say Tristram and when do we say Sterne? Laurence Sterne left tracks in his books as perhaps no other novelist ever has. Walter, Toby, Tristram, Yorick, may all be manifestations of their Creator,[30] but they are certainly manifestations of their creator, and he was a role-player to the last well-dramatized, long-foreseen breath. "The world has imagined," the man tells us, "because I wrote Tristram Shandy, that I was myself more Shandean than I really ever was."[31] But there is simply no telling how Shandean he *really was*. "Really was" simply slides off an old actor like Sterne whose *essence* remained *pure potential*, the power to be anyone. Even the context of the letter whence the just-cited passage discounts it. It is a formal letter, to a nobleman. Sterne is his polite self, the self of the last letters to the Jameses, very much on his p's and q's. As a working distinction, we talk of Tristram when we mean the narrator of *Tristram Shandy* or confine our discussion to the novel. Speaking of the novel as written in a certain time and place, we may use Sterne. And so too of what Tristram does *not see*, his character as satirized.

From among Sterne's perpetual roles, it is useful to precipitate out two at this point, jester and clergyman. Sterne, like Samuel Clemens, found the mask essential, essentially liberating. And it is tempting to see, in Tristram, a discrete mask. To analyze such a mask in Freudian terms, for example, comes so naturally we feel uneasy. The sublimated impotence, the castration complex on every page, now the theme of bastardy Professor Rader has suggested, which would allow Tristram to kill off his father in the story (if Yorick is his father), the importance of infancy and prenatal experience—all come to mind as naturally as

[30] Stedmond, *Comic Art*, p. 53.
[31] Sterne, *Letters*, pp. 402–403.

breathing. I am not competent to pursue this line of investigation. But it is a miracle someone has not done it a bit better than de Froe. Such an analysis would tell us much of Sterne and perhaps even of the novel.[32] I wish to suggest a different train of reasoning, grouping Tristram with the other jester's mask, Yorick, to contrast it with the authentic clergyman's mask. Had we been Sterne's contemporary, we could have seen more clearly the nature of his dual statement about mankind. For the *Sermons* appeared along with *Tristram Shandy* and were, through the figure of Parson Yorick, confusingly tied to the novel. In the *Sermons* Parson Yorick allows his auditors a conventional moral identity. Whatever motive may be, none doubts, in that world, what it should be. Man has a discrete self for which he is totally responsible. The purpose there is frankly rhetorical, to move the will by playing upon the heart. This, precisely, the Tristram mask does not do. *Tristram Shandy* does not teach a conventional ethical lesson, or an absurdist one either. It explicitly denies us a conventional moral identity, makes actors of us all. It makes no statement finally about what we ought to do, but makes a final one about why we do it. It reduces motive to pleasure. It denies us the final moral responsibility high seriousness requires, denies us the tragic self. Tristram is the mask created to scoff at this self. It laughs at our perpetual need to clothe our pleasures with moralizing. It counterstates the *Sermons*. It constitutes Sterne's secular statement. It stands for the self and its needs as the *Sermons* stand for the other. The resemblances between the literary techniques of the two statements are incidental; the difference is fundamental. Sterne the man may well have denied that *Tristram Shandy* works this way. And the commentators seeking high seriousness of whatever kind will certainly do so. But the logic of the narrative structure Tristram creates seems inescapable. In a game world, the only thing you

---

[32] *Tristram Shandy* seems, in fact, almost a book *about* sublimation and the whole Freudian theory of literature.

cannot deny is game, and its only yield and motive is pleasure.

Tristram-Sterne thus takes his place in a distinguished group of narrative masks: The Ovid of the *Ars Amatoria*; Chaucer the Canterbury Pilgrim and the narrator of *Troilus and Criseyde*; Rabelais; the Cervantes of *Don Quixote* if not of the *Novelas Ejemplares*. Like all these nonlovers he is a commentator and observer, a student of ritual, interested more in the psychical structures built on feeling and ideas than in either by itself. And like all, he finally finds the dramatic metaphor for society to prevail, and the role metaphor for individual identity. Whether the attitude toward the play and the roles is loving or savage, whether the observer is amused or horrified, the same reductive attack on the nobility of our motives gets underway. We start shrinking. We begin to feel that particular paralysis creeping over us which perhaps Tristram's game of frenetic activity exists to combat, the paralysis of motive-seeking. Why, if we only play games, bother to play them? What is worth doing? And what framework creates worth? These are Hamlet's questions and Hamlet's paralysis. *Tristram Shandy*'s close and yet puzzling relation to that character and that play suggest some answers.

CHAPTER SEVEN
Parson Yorick & Yorick Hamlet & Tristram Shandy

I

The mask of Yorick sympathetically dramatized Sterne's plight as provincial clergyman with a sensibility and sense of humor beyond the role's demands. It also sold books. The parson with a famous fool's name offended his audience (and later ones) but piqued curiosity and sales. The Yorick in *Tristram Shandy* shilled his part in this sales campaign for the *Sermons*. But he never developed into the obvious role of sacred jester. In a novel full of loose ends, he remains one of the loosest. He never adds up to much. Outside the novel he seems to have been the central mask for Sterne, or at least the mask of everyday. But not in *Tristram Shandy*. To call his parson "Yorick" invites us to use *Hamlet* as gloss for the novel. But the agent extending the invitation stands not so close to the play, or the play's relationships to the novel, as he might. So I split the two, discussing first Parson Yorick in *Tristram Shandy* and then the play's implications for the novel. Sterne issued, through Yorick, three invitations. Compare Parson Yorick and Yorick. More important, compare Tristram and Yorick. Most important, compare Tristram-Sterne and Hamlet. About the relationship of these invitations, Watkins has cautioned:

> Sterne takes his own temperament into account. He certainly did not have Johnson's force of will, but there was a definite

element of choice in his being Yorick rather than Hamlet, Falstaff
rather than Lear . . . he chose deliberately to take the comic view
of life.[1]

Sterne, however, chose to be neither Hamlet nor Yorick in his
greatest novel but a third character tangentially related to both.
How Tristram does *not* play Hamlet we shall see. How Parson
Yorick does not play Yorick hardly needs reflection. Yorick in-
hibits the play by his absence. If Sterne originally conceived
Parson Yorick as picking up where Yorick left off, as adding
once again the range of comic possibility to the Danish court, he
certainly did not develop the idea. Convenient as it would be for
our thesis, he markedly fails to yoke high seriousness and the
pleasure-principle. Yorick's successor as antic wit is Hamlet
himself. And Parson Yorick does not play the central jester's role,
Tristram's role, in the novel. The connection between the two
Yoricks joins play and novel together and then deadends. The
fellow of infinite jest is Tristram.

When capitalizing on chance and chestnut, Yorick plays no
sacramental role.[2] And his latter-day Quixote role (his beginning role in the novel) is hard to accept. Stedmond expresses
the consensus on his portrait:

> Yorick, as we have seen, is presented in *Tristram Shandy* as a
> Cervantic figure, like Uncle Toby a descendent of Don Quixote.
> He has his weaknesses—not the innocence of a Toby (or a Parson
> Adams)—but rather, as Eugenius points out, a blindness to the
> reaction of fools and knaves to witty castigation, and a tendency
> to over-rate the powers of ridicule and plain speaking as a means

---

[1] W. B. C. Watkins, *Perilous Balance* (Princeton, 1939), p. 106.
[2] For the opposite case, see Sigurd Burckhardt: "But, unlike others,
Yorick is willing to pick up the dishonorable object and restore it to dignity
and usefulness." (*"Tristram Shandy's* Law of Gravity," *ELH*, XXVIII
[1961], 86.) On Sterne reviving the role of jester, see also B. H. Lehman,
"Of Time, Personality and the Author, A Study of *Tristram Shandy*:
Comedy," in *Studies in the Comic*, University of California Publications in
English, III, 2 (1941), 238.

of reforming the vicious. Unlike Uncle Toby, he is neither unable nor unwilling to see the flaws in human nature, but he perhaps over-estimates his ability to amend those flaws. However, like Toby, he is essentially good-hearted and benevolent, normally optimistic in his view of the world, and it is this aspect of his character which is brought out in the sermons.[3]

Does not this outline of Yorick show why Sterne never put him center stage? What a close portrait of Sterne, the misunderstood Yorkshire clergyman. How flattering to think of himself as latter-day Quixote, too proud to explain his broken-down Rocinante. And how dripping with self-pity! Poor, misunderstood Yorick. Alas! Yorick stands as Sterne's artistic failure at making a mask, the antithesis of Tristram. In Yorick, Sterne commits the one mistake fatal to humor—he takes himself seriously. Alas, the perpetually misunderstood jester. The connections to Sterne—and to the theme the rest of *Tristram Shandy* artistically shapes—stand out in the introductory portrait. The biographical leading-strings constitute, indeed, the once significant topical reference Sterne did not refine or justify in structural terms. Does not the description of him in Volume I (xii, 26–27) constitute a *description* of the theme the novel *incarnates*?

> —For, to speak the truth, *Yorick* had an invincible dislike and opposition in his nature to gravity;—not to gravity as such;—for where gravity was wanted, he would be the most grave or serious of mortal men for days and weeks together;—but he was an enemy to the affectation of it.
> In the naked temper which a merry heart discovered, he would say, There was no danger,—but to itself:—whereas the very essence of gravity was design, and consequently deceit;—'twas a taught trick to gain credit of the world for more sense and knowledge than a man was worth.

[3] John M. Stedmond, *The Comic Art of Laurence Sterne* (Toronto, 1967), p. 137.

The praise of the guileless candor that follows serves as self-pitying proleptic defense for the novel's well-intentioned iconoclasm. But Sterne's vanity and self-pity seldom conquered his sense of humor in this way. One of *Tristram Shandy's* distinctive additives remains its inclusion, in the portrait of Yorick, of a fundamentally mistaken direction, one that Sterne soon saw as such and did not pursue. By the time we get to the black page (I, xii, 33) and the preceding full-dress sentimental grief for poor dead Yorick, the real mask has killed off the false and is well in control. Tristram has taken over and Parson Yorick is as dead as his namesake.

II

Yorick the sentimental jester seems less likely to have created the long Sermon he authors in the novel than the sly trickster of the chestnut episode. For, far from being the major interjection of pure Sterne into the book, as Stedmond would have it,[4] it stands as the one interjection of alien Sterne, Sterne the moralist, into the domain of Sterne the comic novelist. When the Sermon comes into the game sphere, however, it is hard pressed not to switch allegiance, to take its place among the games of pleasure.

What *Tristram Shandy* really does is reverse the stance of the *Sermons*, declare war on the conscience. For it is the conscience that forces us to adopt postures in which the only enjoyment is feeling itself. I take Sterne's decision to make his parson a Yorick as declaration that, after half a lifetime of sermonizing, he had found the conscience an unpromising way to work his will on his fellow men. Conscience did not tell him what motive was but only what it ought to be. And whatever it was, it proved impossible to move it in any direction toward what it ought to be. The movement from the *Sermons* to *Tristram Shandy* was

---

[4] *Ibid.*, p. 84.

surely a movement from duty to pleasure. Both these largest bodies of Sterne's work deal with what is and what ought to be and how to move from the first to the second. At the center of the concept of man in the first stands Conscience; in the second, Pleasure. By introducing the Sermon on the Abuses of Conscience into *Tristram Shandy* (II, xv, 118 ff.), Tristram brings the two together in order to make us see the vanity of moralizing. The Sermon itself attacks the dependability of the conscience. It does not, we are told, harass us with sufficient consistency and rigor. The pious lesson is positive: would the conscience were more consistent. The literary lesson is negative: the conscience continually collaborates with self-interest, whitewashes what it ought to condemn. It continually deceives us. The Sermon reveals *in extenso* man's infinite sources for self-centered deception. Man, Sterne might say, is a ceaseless seeker after pleasure. Man satisfies himself first. The only sure prop against such deception and hidden self-seeking is revealed truth:

> "Thus conscience, this once able monitor,—placed on high as a judge within us, and intended by our maker as a just and equitable one too,—by an unhappy train of causes and impediments, takes often such imperfect cognizance of what passes,—does its office so negligently,—sometimes so corruptly,—that it is not to be trusted alone; and therefore we find there is a necessity, an absolute necessity of joining another principle with it to aid, if not govern, its determinations.
>
> "So that if you would form a just judgment of what is of infinite importance to you not to be misled in,—namely, in what degree of real merit you stand either as an honest man, an useful citizen, a faithful subject to your king, or a good servant to your God.—call in religion and morality.—" (II, xvii, 132)

He who calls in religion and morality presumably calls the Parson and listens to a Sermon. The listener is likely not to invigorate his conscience with revealed truth but, as Slop does a few lines later, to fall asleep. Or, as Walter Shandy does, savor the rhetoric and relish the doctrinal irregularities that promise a disputation with Slop. Or as Trim does, take an actor's pleasure in delivering it, as his audience takes a theatergoer's pleasure in the hearing. Tristram presents the Sermon as an oration, which it partly is, and includes all suitable accompaniments. In chapter xvii he establishes Trim's *ethos* in great detail of posture and attitude. Then, by the interruptions that follow immediately the beginning of the speech, he establishes the *pathos* or emotional set of the audience equally well. Then he realizes the Sermon in the secular context, brings it home, as one might say, to the Shandy household. Each picks from it whatever is likely to give him pleasure. None harkens after it. They banquet off it. Walter's comment at the end comes not from a reformed sinner but from a rhetorical connoisseur: "Thou hast read the Sermon extremely well, *Trim*" (II, xvii, 140). Then they wonder who wrote it and how it could have gotten into the Stevinus instead of the sailing chariot they had initially sought. What they never discuss is the content of the Sermon. The occasion does not so much undermine or travesty the moral message as render it irrelevant. In the world of *Tristram Shandy* the Parson's role simply does not take. Tristram has supplanted him. This seems the point of introducing the Sermon. The world of ought is another world, and when its techniques of persuasion stray into this one, they can expect this band of tireless pleasure-seekers to make a picnic of them. The Sermon itself *tells* us why sermonizing, endless appeals to the conscience, do not work. Man has endless resources to defeat these appeals. The fictional context in which the Sermon is placed *shows* us why sermonizing does not work. Sermonizing does not aim at the heart of man, at those endless resources of self-deception that protect our pleasures. Sermonizing ignores the resources of game, of self-infatuation, which the scene preceding the Sermon so well illustrates. The opposite kind of attack, that which does aim at the pleasure-seeking heart of man, is the novel itself, of course, *Tris-*

tram Shandy. Tristram does not ask us to put the two roles of Yorick together, to remember the Sermon when we get to the hot chestnut. He does not tell us to notice how the whole appeal of his tale is predicated on a pleading to just that part of man's nature the Sermon ignores. He does not tell us these things, but it is clearly part of his game with us that we should come to see them.

Revealed truth may have been Sterne's answer in life. It is not however an admissible alternative in fiction, limited as it is to the earthly perspectives, and Tristram does not avail himself of it. One might, I suppose, find it suggested here, simply put on the table, much as Chaucer suggests, through Troilus in the eighth sphere, that his poem's perspective is not the only one available to man. Certainly it goes no farther. The rest of the Sermon and its context work to show, at the same time that they show how much man stands to profit from revelation, how thoroughly he fails, by his very nature, to do so. So, far from providing a point of view, either in revealed truth or imperfect conscience, *as a whole,* the episode of the Sermon demonstrates how completely irrelevant each is to the world of *Tristram Shandy.* Tristram makes us play his game out to the end. No shortcuts allowed.

Yorick points to the relationship of *Tristram Shandy* to *Hamlet* but hardly develops it. And the verbal echoes of the play in the novel, although there are a few,[5] would by themselves hardly invite or justify detailed comparison. Echoes of Shakespeare dance in and out of *Tristram Shandy,* but they usually offer themselves context-free, simply as phrases. They seldom veil allusions. We are thrown back on a remarkable similarity in theme and technique between play and novel. Many critics have glossed the strong dramatic strain in *Tristram Shandy,* its working by scene, use of gesture, of prepared speech. Sterne

[5] Some obvious examples: I, x, 23; I, xii, 31; II, x, 107; II, xix, 151; III, xx, 196; V. xii, 368.

made Tristram Shandy as comparable to a play as novel could well be. Both play and novel create radically perplexing worlds, full of purposes mistook fallen on the inventors' heads. In both, to act is to be mistaken, frustrate of one's purpose, compassing purposes never guessed at. Both inquire into motive closely and find it cannot bear the scrutiny. Both come close to the Oedipus-complex in the inquiring. *Hamlet,* like *Tristram Shandy,* is much concerned with role-playing as central to human motivation; they both use, for this end, the play within a play. Both suggest martial honor as finally the least fragile, though the most dangerous, of man's self-sought motives. The kind of socially determined identity we have seen in *Tristram Shandy* Hamlet finds at the bottom of his mystery. Both use an underpinning of bawdy innuendo and both concern themselves greatly with the theme of words. The role of Yorick is unfilled in *Hamlet.* Tristram takes the role and makes of it what Yorick, in Hamlet's world, might have.

Perhaps it will be easiest to begin with war. In the short fourth scene of Act IV, the second quarto has Hamlet deliver himself of a declaration on human motive so puzzling that most producers of the play leave it out altogether. Hamlet has come upon Fortinbras's army and inquires of one of the Captains:

> *Ham.* Good sir, whose powers are these?
> *Cap.* They are of Norway, sir.
> *Ham.* How purposed, sir, I pray you?
> *Cap.* Against some part of Poland.
> *Ham.* Who commands them, sir?
> *Cap.* The nephew to old Norway, Fortinbras.
> *Ham.* Goes it against the main of Poland, sir,
> or for some frontier?
> *Cap.* Truly to speak, and with no addition,
> We go to gain a little patch of ground
> That hath in it no profit but the name.
> To pay five ducats, five, I would not farm it,

> Nor will it yield to Norway or the Pole
> A ranker rate, should it be sold in fee.
>
> *Ham.* Why, then the Polack never will defend it.
> *Cap.* Yes, it is already garrisoned.
> *Ham.* Two thousand souls and twenty thounsand ducats
> Will not debate the question of this straw.
> This is th' imposthume of much wealth and peace.

Hamlet here is perplexed by the power of purely symbolic, purely man-made, motive. He does not respond to it instinctively, as do Fortinbras and Laertes, just as he can hardly believe that Claudius would have committed such a crime only to wear a crown. Again and again Hamlet exhibits the radically discounted analysis of motive which characterizes the private man. In the famous soliloquy that follows this interchange, he lurches back and forth between a rational analysis of motive, his own externally imposed motives of revenge, and the internal honor that moves Fortinbras to so gratuitously bloody a purpose:

> How all occasions do inform against me,
> And spur my dull revenge!

But this shocking reminder of his dulled purpose brings on a fit of self-conscious reflection that tips the scales the other way:

> What is a man,
> If his chief good and market of his time
> Be but to sleep and feed? A beast, no more.
> Sure, he that made us with such large discourse,
> Looking before and after, gave us not
> That capability and godlike reason
> To fust in us unused.

Why, if we are not to reason precisely on the event, if not inquire closely into our motives, were we given reason in the first place? From here, he expands his inquiry into the motive for his own paralysis. He includes forgetfulness and cowardice. He is examining his own mechanism for fooling himself, as indeed he does throughout the play. He then lurches back to the example Fortinbras is setting him:

> Examples gross as earth exhort me.
> Witness this army of such mass and charge,
> Led by a delicate and tender prince,
> Whose spirit, with divine ambition puffed,
> Makes mouths at the invisible event,
> Exposing what is mortal and unsure
> To all that fortune, death, and danger dare,
> Even for an eggshell. Rightly to be great
> Is not to stir without great argument,
> But greatly to find quarrel in a straw
> When honor's at the stake.

Against this, the power of his own motivation should be enormous:

> How stand I then,
> That have a father killed, a mother stained,
> Excitements of my reason and my blood,
> And let all sleep, while to my shame I see
> The imminent death of twenty thousand men
> That for a fantasy and trick of fame
> Go to their graves like beds, fight for a plot
> Whereon the numbers cannot try the cause,
> Which is not tomb enough and continent
> To hide the slain?

The final dedication to bloody purpose ("from this time forth, My thoughts be bloody, or be nothing worth!") should prove that his own motive is the stronger. It does not. The resolution proves fustian. Hamlet goes off peaceably with Rosencrantz and Guildenstern, whereas Fortinbras fights the war. The symbolic purpose proves far stronger than the "real" one. Hamlet, of course, never does carry out his purpose, discharge his overpowering motive. Chance does it for him, just as it rules all else in the play. Honor here I take to be the tragic analogue to the hobbyhorse in *Tristram Shandy*. We laugh at Toby as a comic version of Fortinbras—and we should, since he is a comic character in a comic novel. But clearly we have to do with the same honor, the same kind of symbolic and unreflective purpose.

Many students, most recently Stedmond, have talked about the governing role of chance in *Tristram Shandy*. It plays a precisely analogous one in *Hamlet*. Paralysis is the common word for Hamlet's behavior in the play. Yet he is always being forced to act, as is everyone else in the play. He seems paralyzed because chance supplies both cause and effect. Polonius dies by mistake. Hamlet and Ophelia separate by purposes mistook. Chance turns Laertes's poisoned rapier against himself, puts the poisoned goblet in Gertrude's hand. The soul of Hamlet's heroic response is a Stoical resignation before a universe where to act is to be mistaken: "The readiness is all. . . . Let be." It is possible, I think, to see *Tristram Shandy* as reopening the discussion at this point. In the face of the dominance of chance, you do what Yorick does with the chestnut. You capitalize on it for your own purposes. You cannot thereby control your fate. ("Our thoughts are ours, their ends none of our own.") But at least you can live pleasurably with it. You need not resign yourself to it. The comparison with *Hamlet* shows, it seems to me, the degree to which the novel's final stance is an *active*, not a *passive* one. The jester is not resigned but aggressive. "Let be" is the last thing he would say. He concerns himself not with a cosmic victory but a comic one; not a tragic wrestling with universal fate but a sharp and decisive effort at a self-aware domestic comfort. Surely it is not beyond the bounds of imagination to see Toby's bowling green as the Jester's solution to war and its honor—a decisive translation of it to the game sphere. He domesticates it, puts it in the backyard where it can be disarmed and controlled.

"It is not actions, but opinions concerning actions, which disturb men." This is not far from "there is nothing either good or bad, but thinking makes it so." Both the play and the novel search in vain for things themselves and find only judgments about them. Just as Tristram sees only a series of overlapping games when he tries to make sense of his own experience, to find out what he is and what made him what he is, so Hamlet, when he tries to pierce the arras, finds only a series of plays, finds reality dramatistic, scenically determined. At the beginning of the play he bravely retorts to his mother's inquiry about the seeming particularity of his sorrow:

> Seems, madam! Nay, it is. I know not "seems."
> 'Tis not alone my inky cloak, good mother,
> Nor customary suits of solemn black,
> Nor windy suspiration of forced breath,
> No, nor the fruitful river in the eye,
> Nor the dejected havior of the visage,
> Together with all forms, moods, shapes of grief,
> That can denote me truly. These indeed seem,
> For they are actions that a man might play,
> But I have that within which passeth show,
> These but the trappings and the suits of woe.
>
> [I, ii, 76 ff.]

But he cannot bring it off. He is forced to act out a stage madness. He must play a role to Ophelia. To his mother, he must be cruel to be kind. He tricks Rosencrantz and Guildenstern, plays games with Polonius. Throughout the play he is not what he seems. (And his central role, the revenge-hero, he simply cannot play.) We may find his text, as Sterne found Tristram's, in the *Encheiridion*: "If you undertake rôle which is beyond your powers, you both disgrace yourself in that one, and at the same time neglect the rôle which you might have filled with success."[6] So Hamlet thinks of himself. He has been given a role to play which he is unfitted for: "The time is out of joint: O cursed spite,/ That ever I was born to set it right!" Without implying

[6] *Epictetus*, trans. W. A. Oldfather, 2 vols. (Cambridge, Mass.: Loeb Classical Library, 1966), II, 37.

that we see into the heart of Hamlet's paralysis, we might suggest that he has trouble with taking his role seriously because he is so conscious of role-playing as the basis of human behavior. He has not yet learned the settled acceptance of this aspect of society Epictetus counsels:

> Remember that you are an actor in a play, the character of which is determined by the Playwright: if He wishes the play to be short, it is short; if long, it is long; if He wishes you to play the part of a beggar, remember to act even this role adroitly; and so if your role be that of a cripple, an official, or a layman. For this is your business, to play admirably the role assigned you; but the selection of that role is Another's.

Hamlet's misery is that he cannot play the part given him, as Fortinbras does, nor reason himself into another. Perhaps we can find here his famous modernity; we are taught *not* to accept our parts but to choose them.

Hamlet is obsessed by the ease with which words can create real feeling and substitute for it. He marvels at the Player King's tears:

> Oh, what a rogue and peasant slave am I!
> Is it not monstrous that this player here,
> But in a fiction, in a dream of passion,
> Could force his soul so to his own conceit
> That from her working all his visage wanned,
> Tears in his eyes, distraction in his aspect,
> A broken voice, and his whole function suiting
> With forms to his conceit? And all for nothing,
> For Hecuba!
> What's Hecuba to him, or he to Hecuba,
> That he should weep for her? What would he do
> Had he the motive and the cue for passion
> That I have?
>
> [II, ii, 534 ff.]

He marvels so greatly that he, like the player, fools himself.

> O, vengeance!
> Why, what an ass am I! This is most brave,
> That I, the son of a dear father murdered,
> Prompted to my revenge by heaven and hell,
> Must like a whore unpack my heart with words.
> [II, ii, 567 ff.]

He catches himself acting again. He can reenact a perfect revenge-hero, all except the killing. He puts the lesson the player has taught him to use, however: "the play's the thing / Wherein I'll catch the conscience of the king." One might, in fact, trace Hamlet's inaction to his eloquence, or at least his volubility. He is so good at unpacking his heart with words that he does not need to do the deeds. The words satisfy him. So the Player King:

> I do believe you think what now you speak,
> But what we do determine oft we break.
> Purpose is but the slave to memory,
> Of violent birth, but poor validity,
> Which now like fruit unripe sticks on the tree
> But fall unshaken when they mellow be.
> Most necessary 'tis that we forget
> To pay ourselves what to ourselves is debt.
> What to ourselves in passion we propose
> The passion ending, doth the purpose lose.
> The violence of either grief or joy
> Their own enactures with themselves destroy.
> Where joy most revels, grief doth most lament;
> Grief joys, joy grieves, on slender accident.
> This world is not for aye, nor 'tis not strange
> That even our loves should with our fortunes change.
> [III, ii, 178 ff.]

The trouble is that Hamlet, though he constantly strives to see beyond them, is obsessed with words. He is a poet indeed, and one who runs up against the limitations of language and also its frightening power not only to express and discharge motivation but to create it. Shakespeare seems to make a generic statement. Action and words vary concomitantly as expressions of purpose. If you want to act, keep your mouth shut, like Bolingbroke, the "silent king." This equation seems to govern *Tristram Shandy* too. There can be no real action in the novel. One cannot picture anyone solving anything. The stress is on accommodation to circumstances through words, not on changing circumstances. This is, after all, what Tristram does in writing the story of his life and opinions. He unpacks his heart with words. It is what Walter Shandy does. It is what *we* must do in reading the novel if, as Traugott says, we come up against an impassable barrier in the nature of language itself.

The Victorians exercised themselves a good deal about the sincerity of Laurence Sterne and his various writings. Hamlet, too, wants to penetrate real feeling, true response. Like Bagehot and Thackeray he discovers only imposture and like them he is horrified. He accepts this glum verdict rather than repudiating it and takes refuge in a providence and a Providence that knows the true response from the false, as man does not. It is surprising how almost everyone in the play is loyal to a style of life or pattern of conduct that the play proves false or inadequate. Horatio's Stoicism can come to terms with failure but not with neutral circumstance waiting for a master. Ophelia's filial piety avails nought. Polonius's meddling, loyal officiousness—he is good at his job, contrary to his bad press—leads to a feast where he is eaten rather than eats. Laertes is slave to "honor," yet so blind and thoughtless in following it that he can prate about honor to Hamlet while he holds the poisoned rapier in his hand. Feeling and response seemed to be programmed, not spontaneous. The roles are all ever-so-slightly-too-clearly stage roles: Fortinbras, the brave prince; Laertes, the revenge-hero who *does* act, full of fire; Polonius, the old court gossip; Ophelia, the dutiful maiden; Claudius, the remorseful yet cruel usurper;

Gertrude, the frailty whose name is woman. There is a persistent staginess about *Hamlet* that makes the sincerity question relevant. Sincerity becomes a theme. The modern critic who calls sincerity a red herring in *Tristram Shandy* misses, I think, an essentially similar theme there. When one plays one's role, ceases to worry about it but commits oneself to it as Toby plays at war, then the satisfaction of self which it brings liberates the feelings one can call spontaneous, Toby's sincere fellow-feeling. One has, as Castiglione saw, to *decide* to be spontaneous, to find a spontaneity beyond, not above, affectation.

Hamlet, we may say, labors under a Victorian idea of self. Like the Victorians, he wants it to be autonomous and constant. He is finally unbelieving—not so much shocked as simply unable to believe—in the face of Gertrude's betrayal of his father, just as Chaucer's Troilus cannot believe Criseyde's new affection for Diomede. Though he is an inventive actor and director, he keeps searching for a self beyond the dramatic illusion. Horatio may represent it in the play. Ironically, though, the great apothegm on the matter, Polonius's advice to Laertes to be true to himself, comes at the end of a speech on how to keep up appearances, act an acceptable, decorous role:

> And these few precepts in thy memory
> Look thou character. Give thy thoughts no tongue,
> Nor any unproportioned thought his act.
> Be thou familiar, but by no means vulgar.
> Those friends thou hast, and their adoption tried,
> Grapple them unto thy soul with hoops of steel,
> But do not dull thy palm with entertainment
> Of each new-hatched, unfledged comrade. Beware
> Of entrance to a quarrel; but being in,
> Bear't that the opposed may beware of thee.
> Give every man thy ear, but few thy voice;
> Take each man's censure, but reserve thy judgment.
> Costly thy habit as thy purse can buy,

But not expressed in fancy; rich, not gaudy,
For the apparel oft proclaims the man,
And they in France of the best rank and station
Are of a most select and generous chief in that.
Neither a borrower nor a lender be,
For loan oft loses both itself and friend,
And borrowing dulleth the edge of husbandry.

[I, iii, 58 ff.]

After a character clothed in a pastiche of cliché, we have the marvelous non sequitur: "This above all: to thine own self be true,/ And it must follow as the night the day/ Thou canst not then be false to any man." We might, playing Hamlet ourselves, ask "Self? Self? Self?" (As we might, like Hamlet, kill the man who symbolizes role-playing.) And as for the being false to any man, Laertes is most true to his vengeful role when he is about to kill Hamlet by a trick. Ophelia, too, is most herself—obedient to her father—when she acts as a staked-out heifer, bait to trap Hamlet. And Hamlet himself is closest to his role when most dissembling, when crafty mad. Again and again in the play "truth to self" depends on a self who is not there: truth to role leads to a disastrous, death-dealing self. The way out in *Tristram Shandy* is easier. Live with, turn to pleasure, the inevitable center of dramatistic human experience.

At the end of the play, Fortinbras pronounces a noble epitaph for Hamlet: "For he was likely, had he been put on, / To have proved most royal." We may be permitted to doubt it. Hamlet's sphere, though he is a prince, really is the private life. For he is not willing to act blindly, unless chance impels him, and blind action is the only kind his world permits. The world of *Tristram Shandy* is similarly skeptical, but there one tries not to control events but to enjoy them. This, too, is Hamlet's temptation. He would rather act his revenge out than do it. It is more fun. The tragic view must kill him. The comic view makes of him, we might say, Tristram Shandy.

But close to *Hamlet* as *Tristram Shandy* in many ways is, we must avoid making of the novel a comic version of the play. It is, rather, a comic reply to the world of the play. We see Hamlet's world as Yorick might have seen it. The philosophical humor that modern criticism has seen in the novel seems to me perhaps too close to Hamlet's point of view, a passive endurance rather than a positive response. The Stoic skepticism where *Hamlet* ends is the world where *Tristram Shandy* begins.

A jester is someone who tells us what we ought to do and amuses us in the telling. Tristram does both. What we ought to do, he tells us, is laugh. The pleasure laughter signifies must precede the fellow-feeling he also seeks to recommend. Laughter is, in the novel, synonymous with pleasure. The paths to pleasure, the games of the novel, have been, I hope, made clear. We are amused, finally, by the dramatization of the very pleasure-seeking that it is Tristram's business to recommend. Thus the novel both tells and shows. What it shows is that same exposure of affectation that forms the mainstream of eighteenth-century comedy. Behind all the games is the pursuit of pleasure. This pursuit, it seems to me, and the elaborate deceptions of self and of others that it entails, is the theme of the novel. About it Sterne, and Tristram, take no stand. They do not so much explore the boundary conditions of our understanding as make up a world in which we can be easy. They accept the world as it is and go on from there. After we have mastered the novel's rhetoric, so should we go on. Its didacticism proceeds on a basis of radical disillusionment. It counsels victories that aim to control the self, not the world. The novel's comic acceptance is not desperate. There *is* an optimism at the heart of it. We are not told that mankind can really understand the world. The irrelevance of the question is clearly enough demonstrated. He can, however, understand enough to understand himself, look at himself without blushing, and use his capacity for pleasure to live in the world and enjoy it. The novel is a comedy, but the argument of the comedy is less acceptance than pleasure.

"*Hamlet*," that fine Shakespearean Bernard Shaw tells us, "is the tragedy of private life."[7] We might think of *Tristram Shandy* as the comedy of private life which Sterne erected atop Shakespeare's tragedy. It replies to the play by transcending it. It capitalizes on the philosophical limitations of Hamlet's world, the limitations of words and the drastic limitation of self they reveal. We are tempted at this point to call down God and maintain that Sterne's faith protected him from the despairing conclusions Hamlet could only endure. But it is not so. The protection in *Tristram Shandy* is merely terrestrial and is pleasure. No doubt Sterne was protected. But it does not show in the novel; the novel does not depend on it in any way. The theme of Conscience, knowing and knowing about oneself, leads of its own force in the novel—by virtue of the structure—to Sterne's more optimistic conclusion. The kind of radical forgiveness that ends *Hamlet*, Sterne's novel earns in its own way. The structure that earns it almost seems to ask for the name of tragicomedy. Not because it is blended of happy and sad in an unsatisfactory combination but because Sterne manages to supply us, in pleasure, with a consistent means of distancing ourselves from both. When we go beyond the tragic concept of self, we go beyond pure pathos to the relish of feeling, happy or sad. We thus are prepared, as in a Jacobean tragicomedy, to banquet off feeling. We are prepared to accept Tristram's histrionics as the only alternative to Hamlet's paralysis. Not in the mixture of tragedy and comedy but in the self-conscious attitude toward both does the novel move toward tragicomedy. It accepts its premise, its dedication to effect. Sterne does not say nothing is serious; he

[7] George Bernard Shaw, *Shaw on Shakespeare*, ed. Edwin Wilson (New York, 1961), p. 110.

explores the groundwork of seriousness much rather. Burckhardt has argued brilliantly about Hamlet's central concern:

> I see, then, in *Hamlet*, not so much the bafflement of the poet who cannot find an adequate embodiment for his feelings, but rather the shrinking from the knowledge he has gained. How is he to wrest truth from a medium which has no being apart from the social order and is by this very order corrupted to falsehood?[8]

We are tempted to let *Tristram Shandy* answer this question. It does not. Instead, it argues for changing the venue of Shakespeare's problem. *It makes love to it.* The result of the lovemaking I shall now summarily, somewhat theoretically, attempt to describe.

[8] Sigurd Burckhardt, "The King's Language: Shakespeare's Drama as Social Discovery." *Antioch Review* (Fall 1961), pp. 369–387.

CHAPTER EIGHT
The Magic Circle

Each comedy defines comedy in a new way. And no book, surely, teaches us the vanity of comic dogmatizing better than *Tristram Shandy*. Nothing reminds us more often that definitions are hazardous. For the book seems almost a sampler of comic effect. If it defines its own kind of comedy, it is one composed of many simples. Comedy may perhaps be a serious thing. Sterne's kind, however, so changeable as it is in its theoretical basis, seems calculated to deny this seriousness by denying us a single comic perspective. We laugh first from incongruity, then from sudden glorious superiority, then from relief. Most obviously, the novel makes a reflective statement on the Jonsonian theory of the humors and the corrective satire associated with it. But if Sterne wrote to cure the world of its follies, as he said, and in a Jonsonian way, he was also developing through Toby and his hobbyhorse an antidote to the humor conception of personality, a theory of wit as drawing—and giving—instruction from contrasting humors. Here Hazlitt provides the text: "Humor is the describing the ludicrous as it is in itself; wit is the exposing it, by comparing or contrasting it with something else."[1] We see, in *Tristram Shandy*, humor come to represent

[1] William Hazlitt, *Lectures on the Comic Writers*, I–"On Wit and Humour," *The Collected Works of William Hazlitt*, ed. A. R. Waller and Arnold Glover (London, 1903), VIII, 15.

obsession within the game and wit the game sense, the power that discerns separate games and moves with genial tolerance from one to another. On another terminological pairing, wit and judgment, Tristram also offers theory and practice. The theory comes in the author's preface.

> Now, *Agelastes* (speaking dispraisingly) sayeth, That there may be some wit in it, for aught he knows,—but no judgment at all. And *Triptolemus* and *Phutatorius* agreeing thereto, ask, How is it possible there should? for that wit and judgment in this world never go together; inasmuch as they are two operations differing from each other as wide as east is from west. —So, says *Locke*,—so are farting and hickuping, say I. [III, xx, 193]

Two phases of the same process, they represent, as it were, the antipodes of the psyche. Recalling the dichotomy of rhetoric and philosophy, perhaps we can think of wit as the generalized game sense rhetorical training imparts, judgment as the serious view of man. Pairing in the metaphor, like pairing in the book, yokes opposites in necessary and inevitable connection.

Humor and wit stand as laughed at to laugher. So, too, with the traditional Ciceronian view of the laughable as consisting in *turpitudine et deformitate*. The complement for the laugher is Hobbes's sudden glory. Tristram aims such laughter largely at Dr. Slop and Catholicism. The comic theories clustering round expectation find more extensive illustration in *Tristram Shandy*. Kant's expectation suddenly ending in nothing finds pattern in a dozen promises of deep significance ending with a cock and bull. Quintilian's definition of wit in terms of surprise (*"ut aliter quam est rectum verumque dicatur"*) describes the book's strategy. We see the incongruous precision amid exaggeration comic theorists sometimes discuss. Such seem Walter Shandy's techniques of disputation on the one hand and Toby's battlefield on the other. The one defends exaggerated theses with great precision and finesse; the other fights battles precisely from the dispatches with an exaggeration downward to the homely equipment of old shoes and window weights.

A modern critic points to comedy as self-consciousness about literary illusion: "In tragedy the players on the stage are as objective to the spectators as if they were in a book. But comedy always violates this convention; the actor reaches out of the frame of objectivity and addresses the audience second-personally."[2] And, a page later: "Comedy, violating the stage convention, says 'Ah, but this is only a play.' " Tristram does this continually. The book can be taken as prime document for theories seeing comedy not working through the low style alone, but rather through stylistic contrast. *Tristram Shandy* ranges widely here, from simple literary joking to a philosophic contrast of styles symbolizing larger clusters of feelings and attitudes. Sterne's relation to the older rhetorical narrative patterns constitutes a huge comedy of literary mannerisms and manners. Of *Tristram Shandy* as more conventional comedy of manners evidence abounds. The scale runs from Fielding's "The only source of the true Ridiculous is affectation," to Ovid's "*Quo non ars penetrat?*" Sterne judges by both equally and contradictorily. He posits a normative self and normative manners, mocking all who depart from them. With equal vigor he acts the Visiting Anthropologist. This was the role that so discomfited the Victorians. Their manners were morals. The comedy of manners, as Lamb makes clear in discussing the Victorians' willful misunderstanding, takes an aesthetic view.

We have no such middle emotions as dramatic interests left. . . . We are spectators to a plot or intrigue (not reducible in life to the point of strict morality) and take it all for truth. We substitute a real for a dramatic person, and judge him accordingly. We try him in our courts, from which there is no appeal to the *dramatis personae*, his peers. We have been spoiled with—not

[2] Albert Cook, *The Dark Voyage and the Golden Mean* (New York, 1949), p. 44.

sentimental comedy—but a tyrant far more pernicious to our pleasures . . . the exclusive and all-devouring drama of common life; where the moral point is everything. . . . We carry our fireside concerns to the theatre with us. . . . All that neutral ground of character, which stood between vice and virtue; or which in fact was indifferent to neither, where neither properly was called in question; that happy breathing-place from the burthen of a perpetual moral questioning . . . is broken up and disenfranchised, an injurious to the interests of society.[3]

More eloquent testimonial to the Victorian attack on the spirit of play could hardly be required. Lamb feels the yoke of Arnoldian high-seriousness. Comedy of manners stands opposite this propensity to "love or hate—acquit or condemn—censure or pity—exert our detestable coxcombry of moral judgment upon everything." Thus the Victorians stood precisely equipped to misunderstand Sterne's perspective on man and society, one fundamentally aesthetic, neither moral nor immoral. Amoral. As Bagehot saw, pagan. The sentimental comedy of Sterne's time exhibited, Goldsmith said, the virtues of private life. So *Tristram Shandy*'s ironical sentiment may be seen as a series of scenes from sentimental comedy placed in a matrix from the comedy of manners. The private virtues are put under aesthetic scrutiny.

Comedy, Bergson tells us, is half in life and half out of it.[4] So with Sterne. We can never decide who speaks when and in what mask. Sterne manages to make us think of him and his work as a single body. Although we split off one part for analysis, in the end we must come to terms with the rest. Yorick the clown leads sooner or later to Yorick the preacher. Sterne insists on an unbroken continuum from the most artificial literary pat-

[3] Charles Lamb, "On the Artificial Comedy of the Last Century," *The Essays of Elia and the Last Essays of Elia* (New York, n.d.), pp. 209–210.
[4] Henri Bergson's essay is most conveniently reprinted (as "Laughter") in *Comedy*, ed. Wylie Sypher (New York, 1956), p. 148. This is the edition cited hereafter.

terning to the most spontaneous gesture in life—a broad, uninterrupted reach from style to life style. He argues for the coherence of life and art directly counter to the Victorians' split, yet paradoxically in agreement with it. Lamb divided life and art to save the delicious artificiality of drawing-room comedy. The Victorian mentality would not. Sterne does both, saves the artificiality by calling attention to the artificiality in life.

Bergson's theory of comedy remains, with all its perceptiveness and modifications, romantic humor theory. There is a real self. There is a pattern of behavior natural to it. The natural pattern varies spontaneously. The enemy is mindless repetition. Conventional and affected behavior is inherently unnatural. So wit "consists, for the most part, in seeing things *sub specie theatri*."[5] "It is comic to wander out of one's own self. It is comic to fall into a ready-made category."[6] "The comic expresses, above all else, a special lack of adaptability to society."[7] "We begin, then, to become imitable only when we cease to be ourselves. I mean our gestures can only be imitated in their mechanical uniformity, and therefore exactly in what is alien to our living personality."[8] Finally, "unsociability in the performer and insensibility in the spectator—such, in a word, are the two essential conditions [of comedy].[9] Such a theory, suggestive as it is for *Tristram Shandy*, follows it only part way. Bergson sees that "the comic comes into being just when society and the individual, freed from the worry of self-preservation, begin to regard themselves as works of art."[10] But he does not carry the implications of this self-consciousness to the end. Dramatic perspective attained, we lose our reference point. No norm remains. Every action is an acting. Spontaneity becomes, the more one reaches for it, the more affected. You end up, like Castiglione's Courtier, *affecting* nonchalant spontaneity. Comic correctives evaporate. Comic transcendence becomes problematic.

[5] *Ibid.*, pp. 129–130.   [6] *Ibid.*, p. 157.   [7] *Ibid.*, p. 146.
[8] *Ibid.*, p. 81.   [9] *Ibid.*, pp. 154–155.   [10] *Ibid.*, p. 73.

In sum, the comic frame should enable people *to be observers of themselves, while acting.* Its ultimate would not be *passiveness,* but *maximum consciousness.* One would "transcend" himself by noting his own foibles. He would provide a rationale for locating the irrational and the nonrational.[11]

Unless we greatly mistake it, *Tristram Shandy* destroys such a rationale. It includes and illustrates too many kinds of comedy. Bergson puts his finger on Sterne's basic comic strategy clearly enough. "*A situation is invariably comic when it belongs simultaneously to two altogether independent series of events and is capable of being interpreted in two entirely different meanings at the same time.*"[12] But neither Tristram nor Sterne tells us which meaning is the reference one, which comic theory is to be applied. We can build a comic theory on the postulate of spontaneity, as Bergson did. We can, perhaps more convincingly, build one on repetition, as Kierkegaard does.[13] But what kind of theory will account for a document that builds its comic effects first on one postulate, then on the other? "We have no deeper interest than our integrity," Emerson tells us with his characteristic sobriety, "and that we should be made aware by joke and by stroke of any lie we entertain. Besides, a perception of the Comic seems to be a balance-wheel in our metayphysical structure. It appears to be an essential element in a fine character."[14] But *Tristram Shandy* can be accounted for by no theory of comedy like this, or like Hazlitt's which sees comedy as dramatic ego reducer ("A man cannot be a very great egotist, who every day, sees himself represented on the stage"). *Tristram Shandy* seems to abolish the ego altogether. It does not see

[11] Kenneth Burke, *Attitudes Toward History* (rev. ed., Boston, 1961), p. 171.

[12] Bergson, *Comedy,* p. 123.

[13] See the opening pages of Soren Kierkegaard, *Repetition,* trans. with an introd. by Walter Lowrie (Princeton, 1941).

[14] "The Comic," reprinted in *Theories of Comedy,* ed. Paul Lauter (New York, 1964), p. 380.

comedy as essential to fine character; it eliminates character. The comic therapy may indeed be relief that we need not take seriously something we feared we should have to.

> Properly speaking, then, the comic includes only the ridiculous, the ludicrous, the things which are taken as such by analogy, the witty, and the humorous. All of these, differ as they may, have a common characteristic: their minimization of the claim of some particular thing to be taken seriously, either by reducing that claim to absurdity, or by reducing it merely to the negligible in such a way as to produce pleasure by that very minimization.[15]

But the seriousness *Tristram Shandy* diminishes is the seriousness of the self.

The self persists, if by it we mean Freud's tireless seeker after pleasure. But, under a conception of comedy as dramatic self-consciousness at least, it does not renew its ties to society. It cuts them. The slavery to scene is but a form of slavery to pleasure-seeking self. Here we may quote Schlegel.

> In this respect Comedy bears a very near affinity to Fable: in the Fable we have animals endowed with reason, and in Comedy we have men serving their animal propensities with their understanding. By animal propensities I mean sensuality, or, in a still more general sense, self-love. As heroism and self-sacrifice raise the character to a tragic elevation, so the true comic personages are complete egotists. This must, however, be understood with due limitation: we do not mean that Comedy never portrays the social instincts, only that it invariably represents them as originating in the natural endeavour after our own happiness. Whenever the poet goes beyond this, he leaves the comic tone.[16]

A self then both diminished and enhanced. We surprise this paradox in *Tristram Shandy*: a collection of discrete, forever

---

[15] Elder Olsen, *The Theory of Comedy* (Bloomington, Ind., 1968), p. 23.
[16] "Lectures on Dramatic Art and Literature," trans. John Black, in Lauter, *Theories of Comedy*, p. 346.

colliding selves, but no dependable sense of *self*, all acting and
no action. The comic tone for Schlegel depends on comedy's
keeping "aloof from all moral appreciation of its personages, and
from all deep interest in their fortunes."[17] For "morality, in its
genuine acceptation, is essentially allied to the spirit of Tragedy." Thus we suspect taking comedy seriously in *Tristram
Shandy* to be not inadvisable but impossible. To take Sterne's
comedy seriously is to refuse to take it at all. The serious self is
the sincere self, the social self. Precisely against it comedy rebels.
"What these jokes whisper may be said aloud: that the wishes
and desires of men have a right to make themselves acceptable
alongside of exacting and ruthless morality."[18] The joke, for
Freud, is the contribution of the unconscious to a general theory
of comedy based on pleasure and—even more to the purpose for
Sterne—on pure verbal play as the center and symbol of that
pleasure. Through Freud's comic thesis we may, in fact, be able
to catch the paradoxical self that *Tristram Shandy* both denies
—in its conception of life as absurdist drama—and affirms. If
we are indeed trapped in a self fundamentally dramatic, how
do we know it is real? By its endless pursuit of pleasure. The
very amorality of comedy affirms the self in a way tragedy, for
all its high seriousness, cannot. Comedy thus leads us to entertain what Hamlet could not: "Life is free play fundamentally
and would like to be free play altogether."[19] *Tristram Shandy*
shows us defending ourselves against the pressures of culture
and of instinct by converting them to pleasure. It does not satir-
ize this conversion. Sterne stands it as the center of mortal life.

[17] *Ibid.*, p. 348.
[18] Sigmund Freud, *Jokes and their Relation to the Unconscious*, trans.
James Strachey, 2d ed. (New York, 1960), p. 110.
[19] George Santayana, "Carnival," *Soliloquies in England and Later
Soliloquies* (Ann Arbor, Mich., 1967), p. 141. See also "The Soul at Play,"
in *The Birth of Reason and Other Essays*, ed. Daniel Cory (New York and
London, 1968).

We accept it. We use it. The book begins, after all, by conceiving laughter as defensive gesture.

> Never poor Wight of a Dedicator had less hopes from his Dedication, than I have from this of mine; for it is written in a bye corner of the kingdom, and in a retired thatch'd house, where I live in a constant endeavour to fence against the infirmities of ill health, and other evils of life, by mirth; being firmly persuaded that every time a man smiles,—but much more so, when he laughs, that it adds something to this Fragment of Life.

Tristram Shandy remains rhetorical in this sense: it preserves from the beginning an extraliterary purpose—to keep the spirits up.[20]

I cannot, then, accept the current conception of *Tristram Shandy* as absurdist comedy with sentimental light at the end of the tunnel. Such a view is serious, essentially philosophical. And *Tristram Shandy* is essentially rhetorical, comic. The seriousness the Victorians missed and that the moderns find is tragic seriousness, and it requires a tragic self. "The hero of a tragedy represents an individuality unique of its kind," Bergson tells us.[21] And Susanne Langer: "Tragedy can arise and flourish only where people are aware of individual life as an end in itself, and as a measure of other things."[22] The tragic self and its seriousness *Tristram Shandy* takes pains to deny. They are present on the stage. They form subject, *theme* if you will. But they are denied, not affirmed. *Tristram Shandy* from its pattern-book illustration of comic types does precipitate out a theory, but not one that yields Arnoldian seriousness. It tells us what goes on in the re-

[20] Perhaps this accounts for the varying quality of the book's joking. "It is most instructive to observe how the standards of joking sink as spirits rise. For high spirits replace jokes, just as jokes must try to replace high spirits." (Freud, *Jokes and their Relation to the Unconscious*, p. 127.) Tristram alternates between the two.

[21] Bergson, *Comedy*, p. 166.

[22] Susanne Langer, *Feeling and Form* (New York, 1953), p. 354.

demptive green world. We change selves. Kinds of self. In dealing with the process of changing selves, or in the conflict between the two kinds of self, Sterne goes beyond comedy. He discusses the relation of tragedy and comedy, writes—it is as close as we will allow the word—a "philosophy" of comedy. In thus dealing with this relationship of the two he resumes the ancient quarrel between philosophy and rhetoric. His narrative, like its predecessors in the older tradition of rhetorical narrative, deals with the tradition's central theme, the clash of two fundamentally opposed conceptions of self. How to type such a work, or this long succession of works, perplexes in the extreme. Without arguing about its previous meaning, I am going to appropriate "tragicomedy." Let it refer to the kind of poesy, play, poem, or novel, which takes as artistic subject the relationship between the tragic and comic views of man. This kind of work will both invite us to be serious, as Rabelais does, and Cervantes and Sterne, and mock us for it. It will depict the comic view prevailing, but prevailing by authorial fiat. The author, like Shakespeare at the end of *Measure for Measure*, insists on it by visible, contorted irresolution. Such works will often be didactic: although they show a struggle between the two views, they both show and tell us that the comic should prevail. They are always pushing, as if they were not quite sure the comic view will stick. The struggle against seriousness must never be relaxed. *Tristram Shandy* does not struggle so. Tristram sets up the "Life and Times" format as symbolic of the integral, serious personality, and then never tires—as sometimes we do—of tearing it apart. But Sterne contents himself with showing how the comic does, rather than ought to, prevail.

Tragicomedy, in this definition, always keeps us audience and reminds us of it. No suspension of disbelief. Art remains pageant. It defends a hyperaesthetic view because it must combat a hypoaesthetic one—the intimate moral involvement, the sidelong motion into moral philosophy great tragedy seems always to provoke. Tragedy and comedy differ, among other things, in their attitude toward language. Comedy tends to look *at* it, tragedy *through* it. Our form thus has at its center a stylistic self-consciousness, acute attention to both views of language. Tragedy puts us in the play. Comedy keeps us outside it. Tragicomedy strives to make us see both possibilities as choices.

I said earlier that we could not finally separate the two sides of Sterne's literary production or either side from his clerical self. Perhaps we can now see how they come together. Sterne's religious faith stands, I take it, unquestioned and unquestionable. However he postures to Eliza about his sermons coming "all hot from the heart,"[23] and however Hammond shows them all hot from the library,[24] still they were produced by an extraordinary clergyman with ordinary religious opinions. They, or at least the first four volumes, share several techniques with the two novels[25] but are less remarkable for this than for their time of appearance, their concomitant publication with *Tristram Shandy*.[26] We have our choice. We may think of Sterne's saying essentially the same thing, but in two different ways, in the two publications. Margaret Shaw, I suppose, expresses this position best:

> To consider Sterne's Shandean Philosophy apart from the teaching of his sermons is a mistake that too many critics have made. The two, in fact, are complementary to each other. Interpreta-

[23] Laurence Sterne, *Letters of Laurence Sterne*, ed. Lewis C. Curtis (Oxford, 1935), p. 298.

[24] Lansing vander Leyden Hammond, *Laurence Sterne's Sermons of Mr. Yorick* (New Haven, 1948).

[25] "In the four earlier-published volumes, on the other hand, the majority of discourses could have been composed by no one but Yorick. Here one constantly encounters most of the features which made *Tristram Shandy* and *A Sentimental Journey* so distinctive: the same ability to conceive dialogue, create characters, and furnish a scene with sharply etched backgrounds; the digressions and the eccentricities of punctuation; the obvious delight in alternately shocking and then moving people to tears by deft portrayals of the soft and delicate states of emotion." Hammond, *Laurence Sterne's Sermons*, p. 45.

[26] See John M. Stedmond, *The Comic Art of Laurence Sterne* (Toronto, 1967), p. 135.

tions of the same conception of truth as lying betwixt extremes of error, but differently expressed to serve their separate ends, the straightforward pronouncements on the nature of good and evil in Yorick's discourses and the paradoxical humour of Tristram's opinions combine to form a picture of man in all his aspects, spiritual, intellectual and physical alike. In the sermons, laying especial emphasis on the heart as the mainspring of actions in accordance with or contrary to the principles of Christian religion, Sterne gives a clear and serious account of the passions that lead men astray: in his novel, chiefly concerned with the head as the source of rational and irrational opinions, he deliberately chooses a less grave and orderly means of presentation, the better to awaken laughter at the capricious variations of sense and nonsense in the brain.[27]

Tristram Shandy becomes, in this view, a kind of extended, free-wheeling sermon on the text: "the principal spirit in the Universe is one of joy."[28] Thinking Sterne a philosopher of the sentimental absurd essentially extends this view. Critical respectability comes with a much closer analysis of the novel as a verbal structure, but the philosophical arena of the novel—and its conception of the human heart—remains that of the *Sermons* minus God. The cure for our problems remains in fellow-feeling, in sentiment rightly construed and bravely applauded.

Another interpretation offers itself. We may think of the two statements, sermon and novel, as fundamentally different in kind and intention. Here is Sterne himself on preaching:

> Preaching (you must know) is a theologic flap upon the heart, as the dunning for a promise is a political flap upon the memory:— both the one and the other is useless where men have *wit enough* to be honest.[29]

[27] Margaret R. B. Shaw, *Laurence Sterne: The Making of a Humorist, 1713–1762* (London, 1957) p. 112–113.
[28] W. B. C. Watkins, *Perilous Balance* (Princeton, 1939), p. 118.
[29] Sterne, *Letters*, p. 134.

Surely *Tristram Shandy's paideia* of the reader's imagination premises that man has wit enough to be honest. (In the sermons, however, Sterne preaches to the gluttons of sensual delight.)[30] The book declares Sterne's independence from the need to write sermons. He allows himself a secular mode, and this mode, this pagan *consolatio*, has its own rules and implications. In the sermons, Sterne presents himself again and again as literary critic of the sacred text. In *Tristram Shandy*, the text has become a secular, even a profane, one. The *Sermons* tell us repeatedly that the path of righteousness is the path of joy: "good is that which can only give the mind pleasure and comfort—and . . . evil is that, which must necessarily be attended sooner or later with shame and sorrow."[31] Religion is calculated to make us happy in this life, as in the next. God bids us enjoy life.[32] And the path of truth and knowledge leads to joy too:

> There is nothing generally in which our happiness and honour are more nearly concerned, than in forming true notions both of men and things.[33]

Here, in the *Sermons*, we can find the dependable center of Laurence Sterne's optimism. But we cannot automatically transfer it to the novel because so much in the novel seems to recall these passages in the *Sermons*, so many of the techniques seem to be the same. True notions of men *sub specie aeternitatis* are not those of man *sub specie ludi*. Sterne's *Sermons* do betray remarkable optimism and faith. The novel deliberately does without both. Coming to it from reading the *Sermons* is like plunging into a cold bath. The reassurance is gone. The comfortable, traditional conception of moral identity, so reassuring

---

[30] Sterne, *The Sermons of Mr. Yorick*, Clonmel ed., (New York and London, 1904), no. XXIX.
[31] *Ibid.*, no. XXVIII.
[32] *Ibid.*, no. XXXVII.
[33] *Ibid.*, no. XIX.

in the *Sermons*,[34] vanishes. We have instead the chilly paganism
Bagehot noticed, the Stoicism of Hamlet and Horatio. Moralizing is everywhere, but no moral anywhere. Instead of the firm
conviction that reason and feeling go on together, and that both
jump with the humor of God, we have feeling ironically qualified, sentiment scrutinized, reason attacked.[35] In the novel,
Sterne may be ventilating the many doubts that a lifetime of
sermonizing reassurance in others had created in himself. But
however our biographical guesswork runs, he certainly tests all
the sermons' assumptions by secular experience. He supplies not
a complementary—or a complimentary—but a counter statement.

The only way out of the novel's radical skepticism lies through
religious belief, and we are as free to take it as Sterne was. Huizinga puts the relation of the two domains in the most general
terms:

> The human mind can only disengage itself from the magic circle
> of play by turning towards the ultimate. Logical thinking does not
> go far enough. Surveying all the treasures of the mind and all
> the splendours of its achievements we shall still find, at the bot-
> tom of every serious judgement, something problematical left. In
> our heart of hearts we know that none of our pronouncements
> is absolutely conclusive. At that point, where our judgement be-
> gins to waver, the feeling that the world is serious after all wavers
> with it. Instead of the old saw: "All is vanity," the more posi-
> tive conclusion forces itself upon us that "all is play."[36]

We are free to break out of the magic circle in *Tristram Shandy,*
and if we choose to do so, a very different reading will result.
But nothing in the novel invites us to break out or shows us a
way to. *We* must supply both the inclination and the direction.

[34] Although not altogether unexamined: see *ibid.*, no XVII.
[35] On the attack on reason, see Robert A. Donovan, *The Shaping Vision:
Imagination in the English Novel from Defoe to Dickens* (Ithaca, N.Y.,
1966), p. 112.
[36] J. Huizinga, *Homo Ludens* (Boston, 1955), p. 212.

The form of the fiction works not to favor such an inclination but to discourage it. It is Eros that supplies the obvious link between the two selves, opens the circle, and precisely this Sterne chose to leave out of his book. *Tristram Shandy* does not create a universe suffused with grinning existential despair, but full of tireless pleasure-seekers and inexhaustible sources of pleasure. About this search, Sterne says nothing. (Tristram is, of course, all for it.) He simply reports it. He is far less intrusive a moralist than Freud, for example, far less a champion of reason. In disposing of the enemies of reason, Freud finally comes not to passion but the conscience as the last and greatest enemy. Sterne simply, via the sermon, throws conscience on the banquet table of pleasure along with everything else, and observes the feast.

If there is an unexposed root assumption in the novel, it is not that the principle of the universe is one of joy, "Tochter aus Elisium," but rather that consciousness is good. Awareness is more likely to make people good than bad. Sterne, unlike Shakespeare, seems to have had no nightmares about this assumption. He dreamed no Iagos. Historically, such an assumption can hardly be sustained; but in the sphere of the private life, perhaps. One is continually tempted by the great suggestiveness of the form of *Tristram Shandy* to force from it statements about the public life. It makes none. It is tempting, for example, to argue that all the novel's play with formal rhetorical theory satirizes the public life that rhetorical theory so nicely symbolizes. But finally the satire is so mild it may not be there at all. Sterne simply introduces all that theory into the domain of private life and watches his characters sport with it. Its character, nature, whatever, in the public sphere is plainly irrelevant. A strong strand of "Yorkshire Epic" commentary runs through Sterne criticism. Can we take over this strand and make of the novel an epic treatment of the narrowest and yet the broadest locale of all, the private life? Surely it is not Yorkshire, or Shandy

Hall Sterne talks of but Home and Garden. The uniqueness, singularity of Shandy Hall which he is forever pointing to stands for the uniqueness of home to each of us. Which of us, faced with the need to explain *our* family, would not fall back on Tristram's clichés of singularity?[37]

If we read the novel in this way, we go some distance toward bringing together those who find the Sterne of the *Sermons* in *Tristram Shandy* and those who might follow this essay's argument. Sterne explores the resources of pleasure to be found in the private life. The novel analyzes the private life. But it does not say this is all of human experience. Nor does it offer advice on what to do once we have anatomized the private life in this way. It is a closed system. It is violently reductive of human motive. It is full of implications. But, as the history of Sterne criticism amply proves, each will pursue the implications of his choice. Each will grab his own handle. This is a matter of supreme indifference—no, perhaps, of amused indifference—to Sterne. It confirms his point. The boundary of his ambition was a book where ambition was irrelevant. He aimed to measure not accomplishment but contentment. It is the *nature* of the private life to seek pleasure. This is Sterne's point and the novel's. What ethical or passionate cathedrals the reader chooses to build on this rock are his own business. He can reproach with the Victorians, philosophize with the moderns, believe with the pious, laugh his own laughter.

The novel thus philosophizes the relation of humor to wit, and of both to satisfaction. It provides a pleasure equation of mutual tolerance for the private life. But it philosophizes little else. It does not tell us that, if we ponder role-playing long enough, we shall find a role that is really us. It does not find motive unfathomable. It supplies pleasure at the bottom and proves its valence. It does not tell us how to endure time and chance but

[37] Thus Lewis Curtis: "*Tristram Shandy* . . . a truly great novel of domesticity." *Letters*, xxxi.

how to play games with them, capitalize on them, make them our own.

Ritual and game do the job beautifully, with great economy and precision. There is no other theme. Procreation and everything else graze in the same pasture, and they share it with the cock and bull fertility symbols Sterne borrowed from the frontispiece to his Burton.[38] They are all fair game; we banquet on them all equally. If, at the novel's close, we have come to see this, it has done its work, supplied a *paideia* for our imagination according to the pleasure principle. We have, like Uncle Toby, gone to school in obsession, learned the motives that engross us, and full of this newfound knowledge, we are, like him, ready to feel.

---

[38] The frontispiece had ten panels, with an argument for each. Here is the one for number two.

> To the left a landscape of Jealousie,
> Presents itself into thine eye
> A kingfisher, a swan, a hern,
> Two fighting-cocks you may discern,
> Two roaring bulls each other hie,
> To assault concerning venery
> Symbols are these; I say no more,
> Conceive the rest by that's afore.

Works Cited

Axelos, Kostas. *Le Jeu du Monde.* Paris: Editions de Minuit, 1969.
———. *Vers la Pensée Planétaire.* Paris: Editions de Minuit, 1964.
Bagehot, Walter. *Literary Studies.* Ed. R. H. Hutton. 2 vols. London:
    J. M. Dent & Sons, 1916.
Beaujour, Michel. *Le Jeu de Rabelais.* Editions de l'Herne, n.p., n.d.
———. "The Game of Poetics." *Yale French Studies.* Vol. 41.
Benveniste, Émile. "Le Jeu comme structure." *Deucalion,* no. 2
    (1947).
Bergson, Henri. "Laughter." *Comedy.* Ed. Wylie Sypher. New York:
    Doubleday & Sons (Doubleday Anchor Books), 1956.
Berne, Eric. *Games People Play.* New York: Grove Press, 1964.
Black, Duncan. "The Unity of Political and Economic Science."
    The Economic Journal (September, 1950).
Booth, Wayne C. Review of Ernest N. Dilworth, *The Unsentimental
    Journey of Laurence Sterne* (New York, 1948). *MP,* vol.
    XLVI (1949).
———. "The Self-Conscious Narrator in Comic Fiction before *Tristram
    Shandy.*" *PMLA,* vol. LXVII (1952).
Burckhardt, Sigurd. "The King's Language: Shakespeare's Drama as
    Social Discovery." *Antioch Review* (Fall 1961).
———. "*Tristram Shandy*'s Law of Gravity." *ELH,* vol. XXVIII
    (1961).

Burke, Kenneth. *Attitudes Toward History.* Rev. ed. Boston: Beacon Press (Beacon Paperback), 1961.

———. *Counter-Statement.* 2d. ed. Chicago: University of Chicago Press (Phoenix Paperback), 1957.

Caillois, Roger. *Man, Play and Games.* Trans. Meyer Barash. New York: Free Press of Glencoe, 1961.

Cash, Arthur J. *Sterne's Comedy of Moral Sentiments: The Ethical Dimension of the "Journey."* Pittsburgh: Duquesne University Press, 1966.

———. "The Sermon in *Tristram Shandy.*" *ELH*, vol. XXXI (1964).

Connolly, Cyril. "Sterne and Swift." *Atlantic Monthly*, vol. CLXXV (June, 1945).

Cook, Albert. *The Dark Voyage and the Golden Mean.* New York: Norton & Co. (Norton Library Paperback), 1949.

Daiches, David. *A Critical History of English Literature.* 2 vols. London: Secker & Warburg, 1960.

De Froe, A. *Laurence Sterne and His Novels Studied in the Light of Modern Psychology.* Groningen: P. Noordhoff, 1925.

Dilworth, Ernest N. *The Unsentimental Journey of Laurence Sterne.* New York: King's Crown Press, 1948.

Donovan, Robert A. *The Shaping Vision: Imagination in the English Novel from Defoe to Dickens.* Ithaca, N.Y.: Cornell University Press, 1966.

Drew, Elizabeth. *The Novel: A Modern Guide to Fifteen English Masterpieces.* New York: Dell Publishing Co., 1963.

Ehrmann, R. "*Homo Ludens* Revisited." *Yale French Studies.* Vol. 41.

Epictetus. *Epictetus.* Trans. W. A. Oldfather. 2 vols. Cambridge: Loeb Classical Library, 1966.

Farrell, William J. "Nature Versus Art as a Comic Pattern in *Tristram Shandy.*" *ELH*, vol. XXX (1963).

Fluchère, Henri. *Laurence Sterne, de l'homme à l'oeuvre.* Paris: Gallimard, 1961.

Freud, Sigmund. *Jokes and Their Relation to the Unconscious.* Trans. James Strachey. 2d. ed. New York: Norton & Co. (Norton Library Paperback), 1960.

Frye, Northrop. "Toward Defining an Age of Sensibility." *Eighteenth*

Century English Literature. Ed. James L. Clifford. New York: Oxford University Press (Galaxy Paperback), 1959.

Glaesner, H. "Laurence Sterne," *TLS* (1927) pp. 361–362.

Hall, Joan Joffe. "The Hobbyhorsical World of *Tristram Shandy*." *MLQ*, vol. XXIV (1963).

Hammond, Lansing vander Leyden. *Laurence Sterne's Sermons of Mr. Yorick*. New Haven: Yale University Press, 1948.

Hartley, Lodwick. *Laurence Sterne in the Twentieth Century*. Chapel Hill: University of North Carolina Press, 1966.

Hazlitt, William. *The Collected Works of William Hazlitt*. Ed. A. R. Waller and Arnold Glover. London: J. M. Dent & Co., 1902–06.

Hine, Reginald L., F. S. A. Letter to *TLS* (1931), p. 408.

Holland, Norman O. "The Laughter of Laurence Sterne." *Hudson Review*, vol. IX (1956).

Hooker, Edward N. "Humour in the Age of Pope." *HLQ*, vol. XI (1948).

Houghton, Walter E. Jr. "The English Virtuoso in the Seventeenth Century." *JHI*, vol. III (1942).

Howes, Alan B. *Yorick and the Critics: Sterne's Reputation in England, 1760–1868*. New Haven: Yale Universtiy Press, 1958.

Huizinga, J. *Homo Ludens*. Boston: Beacon Press (Beacon Paperback), 1955.

————. *In the Shadow of Tomorrow*. New York: Norton & Co. (Norton Library Paperback), 1964 [1936].

Jaeger, Werner. *Paideia: The Ideals of Greek Culture*. Trans. Gilbert Highet. 3 vols. Oxford: Basil Blackwell, 1965.

Jefferson, D. W. "*Tristram Shandy* and the Tradition of Learned Wit." *Essays in Criticism*, vol. I (1951).

Kennedy, George. *The Art of Persuasion in Greece*. Princeton: Princeton University Press, 1963.

Kenner, Hugh. *Flaubert, Joyce and Beckett, The Stoic Comedians*. Boston: Beacon Press, 1962.

Kerr, Walter. *Tragedy and Comedy*. New York: Simon & Schuster (Clarion Paperback), 1967.

Kierkegaard, Soren. *Repetition*. Trans. Walter Lowrie. Princeton: Princeton University Press, 1941.

Lamb, Charles. "On the Artificial Comedy of the Last Century." *The Essays of Elia* and the *Last Essays of Elia*. New York: Doubleday & Co. (Dolphin Paperback), n.d.

Langer, Susanne. *Feeling and Form*. New York: Charles Scribner's Sons (Scribner Library Paperback), 1953.

Lanham, Richard A. "Games, Play, and High Seriousness in Chaucer's Poetry." *English Studies*, vol. XLVIII (1967).

Lauter, Paul, ed. *Theories of Comedy*. New York: Doubleday & Sons (Doubleday Anchor Book), 1964.

Lehman, B. H. "Of Time, Personality and the Author, A Study of *Tristram Shandy*: Comedy." *Studies in the Comic*, University of California Publications in English, vol. III, no. 2 (1941).

Lockridge, Ernest H. "A Vision of the Sentimental Absurd: Sterne and Camus." *Sewanee Review*, vol. LXXII (1964).

Maack, Rudolph. *Laurence Sterne im Lichte seine Zeit*. Hamburg: Friederischen, de Gruyter & Co., 1936.

Mayoux, Jean-Jacques. "Laurence Sterne." (Original title: "Laurence Sterne parmi nous," *Critique: Revue générale des publications françaises et étrangères*, XVIII, 177 [February, 1962], 99–120.) Trans. John Traugott. Reprinted in *Laurence Sterne: A Collection of Critical Essays*. Ed. John Traugott. Englewood Cliffs, N.J.: Prentice-Hall (Spectrum Paperback), 1968.

McKillop, Alan D. *The Early Masters of English Fiction*. Lawrence: University of Kansas Press, 1956.

Olsen, Elder. *The Theory of Comedy*. Bloomington: Indiana University Press, 1968.

Ong, Walter J., S. J. *The Presence of the Word*. New Haven: Yale University Press, 1967.

Piper, William Bowman. *Laurence Sterne*. New York: Twayne Publishers, 1965.

Plato. *Philebus*. Trans. R. Hackforth. *The Collected Dialogues of Plato*. Ed. Edith Hamilton and Huntington Cairns. New York: Pantheon Books (Bollingen Series LXXI), 1961.

Pope-Hennessy, Dame Una. "Laurence Sterne." *The Quarterly Review*, vol. CCLXVI (January, 1936).

Price, Martin. *To the Palace of Wisdom*. Garden City, N.Y.: Doubleday & Co., 1964.

Priestley, J. B. *The English Comic Characters.* New York: Dodd, Mead & Co., 1925.

Rapoport, Anatol. *Fights, Games, and Debates.* Ann Arbor: University of Michigan Press, 1960.

———.*Two-Person Game Theory: The Essential Ideas.* Ann Arbor: University of Michigan Press, 1966.

Read, Herbert. *The Sense of Glory.* Cambridge: Cambridge University Press, 1929.

Reid, Ben. "The Sad Hilarity of Sterne." *Virginia Quarterly Review,* vol. XXXII (1956).

Roberts, John M., Malcolm J. Arth, and Robert R. Bush. "Games and Culture." *American Anthropologist,* n.s. vol. 61 (1959).

Rose, H. J. *A Handbook of Latin Literature.* 3d. ed. London: Methuen & Co., 1961.

Saintsbury, George. *Prefaces and Essays.* London: Macmillan & Co., 1933.

Santayana, George. *Soliloquies in England* and *Later Soliloquies.* Ann Arbor: University of Michigan Press (Ann Arbor Paperback), 1967.

———. *The Birth of Reason.* Ed. Daniel Cory. New York and London: Columbia University Press, 1968.

Scholes, Robert, and Robert Kellogg. *The Nature of Narrative.* New York: Oxford University Press, 1966.

Scott, Sir Walter. *Sir Walter Scott: On Novelists and Fiction.* Ed. Ioan Williams. London: Routledge & Kegan Paul, 1968.

Segal, Charles P. "Gorgias and the Psychology of the Logos." *Harvard Studies in Classical Philology,* vol. 66 (1962).

Shaw, George Bernard. *Shaw on Shakespeare.* Ed. Edwin Wilson. New York: E. P. Dutton & Co. (Dutton Paperback), 1961.

Shaw, Margaret R. B. *Laurence Sterne: The Making of a Humourist, 1713–1762.* London: Richards Press, 1957.

Shubik, Martin, ed. *Game Theory and Related Approaches to Social Behavior.* New York: Wiley & Co., 1964.

Stedmond, John M. *The Comic Art of Laurence Sterne.* Toronto: University of Toronto Press, 1967.

Stephen, Sir Leslie. *English Literature and Society in the Eighteenth Century.* London: Duckworth, 1940.

Sterne, Laurence. *Letters of Laurence Sterne.* Ed. Lewis P. Curtis. Oxford: Oxford University Press, 1935.

——. *The Life and Opinions of Tristram Shandy, Gentleman.* Ed. James A. Work. New York: Odyssey Press, 1940.

——. *The Sermons of Mr. Yorick.* New York and London: The Clonmel Society, 1904.

Thackeray, W. M. *The English Humourists of the Eighteenth Century.* New York: Harper & Bros., 1853.

Towers, A. R. "Sterne's Cock and Bull Story." *ELH*, vol. XXIV (1957).

Traugott, John, ed. *Laurence Sterne: A Collection of Critical Essays.* Englewood Cliffs, N.J.: Prentice-Hall (Spectrum Paperback), 1968.

——. *Tristram Shandy's World: Sterne's Philosophic Rhetoric.* Berkeley and Los Angeles: University of California Press, 1954.

Van Ghent, Dorothy. *The English Novel: Form and Function.* New York: Harper & Row (Harper Torchbook), 1961.

Vaughan, C. E. "Sterne and the Novel of His Times." *Cambridge History of English Literature*, vol. 10. Cambridge: Cambridge University Press, 1913.

von Neumann, J., and O. Morgenstern. *Theory of Games and Economic Behavior.* Princeton: Princeton University Press, 1947.

Wasserman, Earl R. *The Subtler Language.* Baltimore, Md.: The Johns Hopkins Press, 1959.

Watkins, W. B. C. *A Perilous Balance.* Princeton: Princeton University Press, 1939.